THE

Wait

WILL NOT BE

Wasted

LAUREN LIANNE

THE *Wait* WILL NOT BE *Wasted*

LEARNING TO
TRUST GOD'S PLAN
FOR YOUR SEASON
OF SINGLENESS

REDEMPTION P
PRESS

Published by Redemption Press, PO Box 427, Enumclaw, WA 98022.

Toll-Free (844) 2REDEEM (273-3336)

Redemption Press is honored to present this title in partnership with the author. The views expressed or implied in this work are those of the author. Redemption Press provides our imprint seal representing design excellence, creative content, and high-quality production.

Scripture quotations marked CEB are taken from the Common English Bible. © Copyright 2011 by the Common English Bible. All rights reserved. Used by permission.

Scripture quotations marked MSG are taken from The Message, copyright © 1993, 2002, 2018 by Eugene H. Peterson. Used by permission of NavPress. All rights reserved. Represented by Tyndale House Publishers, Inc.

Scripture quotations marked NIV are taken from the Holy Bible, New International Version®, NIV® Copyright ©1973, 1978, 1984, 2011 by Biblica, Inc.® Used by permission. All rights reserved worldwide.

Unless otherwise indicated, all Scripture quotations are taken from the Holy Bible, New Living Translation, copyright © 1996, 2004, 2015 by Tyndale House Foundation. Used by permission of Tyndale House Publishers, Inc., Carol Stream, Illinois 60188. All rights reserved.

ISBN 13: 978-1-64645-031-2 (Paperback)
         978-1-64645-032-9 (ePub)
         978-1-64645-033-6 (Mobi)

Library of Congress Catalog Card Number: 2020902123

To each and every woman who has
ever felt forgotten or somehow
less than because you aren't married yet.
This is for you.

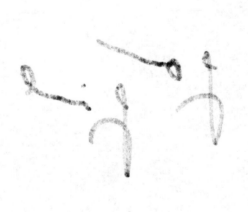

Contents

Preface

*I*f you are holding this book in your hands, I want you to know I already consider you a friend. And before we even get started, there are some things I want you to know.

First of all, I'm so sorry you are here and are a part of this singles club. In case no one has ever told you that before, know that I am validating the hard. I wish things had gone differently for both of us. I know your hurt, and I've felt your pain. But somehow I'm also really thankful you have found yourself in this season. There is something so sacred and special about this journey we both share. I'm so very different because of this season, and I feel so much closer to Jesus. I'm praying that you will one day be able to say the same thing as well!

I've heard all the things before, as I'm sure you have too. *Just enjoy your singleness; it won't last forever. Just stop worrying about your husband, and he'll come when you least expect it.* I know people mean well when they say these things, but I also know they are not what you want to hear. And they have most likely not brought much comfort to your hurting heart. I'm really hoping the words on these pages will feel different and will help bring some of the healing your heart desperately needs.

I hate that at some point you've probably felt less than or that something is wrong with you because you aren't married yet. Somehow marriage has become kind of a benchmark of success and worthiness. It seems like we often believe that the people who have gotten married somehow deserve it more or have done something more right. But the truth is there isn't one of us that deserves or has earned anything good we have in our lives. Everything we have is a gift from our heavenly Father. I want you to know you are seen, chosen, and so very loved right where you are. Even if you are married, single, divorced, or widowed, that will never change. Your heavenly Father knows everything about you and loves you with the kind of love that is hard for our human minds to even understand.

I also want you to know I don't feel qualified to deliver this message. But I think that has always been the point—without Jesus none of us are qualified, but He chooses to use us anyway. I didn't want to be here, and in a lot of ways, I didn't ask for this. When I first started writing this book, I really wanted it to be about waiting in general, and I wanted to avoid its being associated with my singleness. But as I began to write, it became clear that you had my heart, and you were who I found myself writing to. Singleness is my lane, and even though I don't always love it, I'm walking forward and believing God can use it. It has become clear to me I needed to write these words, and the Lord even used them as such timely reminders as I was editing them. Turns out I needed my own advice. This book has truly become my act of worship and my thank-you to God for how far He has brought me. I've seen what a mess I am without Him, and I'm so thankful for His grace. I most definitely am a human who needs a lot of grace.

Just a heads-up, I tried to get as detailed and as vulnerable as possible. I don't always love it in the moment, but I've learned the value of vulnerability. I know it can be the birthplace of hope and freedom. Know that I've already prayed for that for you. I hope you can feel the freedom to experience all of your hurt and disappointment and you will begin to discover God is right in the middle of your pain with you.

I wish I were sitting across from you at your favorite coffee shop right now. I wouldn't be ordering any coffee (I'm not a fan), but I would love to sit there with you all the same. I would ask you to share your story, and because I love details so much, I'd ask you to leave nothing out. We would most likely laugh and also cry, and we would end up feeling like we have been friends forever. There would be this deep understanding between the two of us, and this would shed some light into the darkest corners of our hearts. This wait that we both know so well is a sensitive subject for both of us, but somehow being able to encourage each other would bring so much hope and peace. We would take great comfort knowing another human understands what it feels like for our deepest desire not to be met yet.

Even though we aren't sitting across from each other, know I am still praying that the words in this book bring the same spark of hope, that you realize you are not alone in your desires or your struggles, and that you no longer feel shame for them or feel like you have to hide them. I'm also praying you come to know not a moment of your wait will be wasted. You can cling to the fact your suffering will not be in vain. God will redeem all of it, and He will make sure every bit of the hard is used for good. He is in the waiting.

A few logistical things … atthings: at the end of each chapter you will find a "Let's Get Real" section. These are going to be some questions to think about and some prayers to help guide you in your time with the Lord. I pray as you work through this section, it will feel messy and personal. I hope answering those questions will be a sacred space with you and Jesus where you can be really honest. This isn't a test and there are no grades or points given out, so no need to try to give the polished answer. "Let's Get Real" with where we actually are, so we can more easily see the places in our lives that need some extra attention. If God brings things to your mind, He isn't doing it to throw it in your face or to make you feel bad. He's bringing it up because He loves you and He wants you to walk in total healing and freedom. If nothing immediately comes to mind or you are not sure of an answer, all you have to do is ask. The Holy Spirit longs to speak to us and show us things. Also make sure you grab a journal of some sorts so you can write everything down. You will quickly learn how much I love being able to look back at all God has done and I believe you will too. Writing it down also gets things out of our heads and hearts, which can be vital to our healing!

I believe in you, and I believe your story matters. I believe the Lord has so many wonderful things for you to accomplish right here and right now. Even as you wait. I'm praying the world gets to see the best you possible. We need you.

Xoxo,

Lauren

Acknowledgments

This list is tangible proof of the lavish love of my Father. I'm so thankful.

To all my girls who called me an author before I was even willing to call myself one: thank you. Your calls, texts, ideas, and constant encouragement kept me going on the days the Enemy tried to convince me that putting myself out there wasn't worth the risk. This book is a reality because of you. Thank you for fighting with me and for me. Each of you at one point or another has chosen to step into the darkness with me, and that has changed everything. Thank you for walking this road with me. It's not always easy admitting that I have needs, but each of you has been a safe place to be my full self. I'm so grateful.

To my fam: I think my beloved counselor said it best: "Your family is so resilient." I know firsthand that is so true. Life has not always been the easiest, but we have always stuck together through it all. Being a part of such resilience and strength helped make me the person I am today.

Mom: I miss you every day, but I know in the deepest parts of me that you would be so crazy proud. You would be telling everyone you knew about this book and would want to know every single detail. I miss your laugh and your hugs, and I even miss the way you would always call and ask for boy updates. Thank you for reminding us all that even during the worst situations, God is still good and there is always something to be thankful for. You fought so long and hard to stay here with us, I'll never have to question how much I was loved. You were such a soldier, and I pray your legacy will go on and on. You were the best kind of mother, and I'm forever grateful you were mine!

Dad: Thank you for believing in my craziest dreams and always encouraging me to follow my heart. I dream big dreams because of you, and you taught me with Jesus anything is possible. I've never had to question if you loved me or if you were proud of me. You've always been so quick to encourage me, and you've never stopped being my biggest fan. A girl needs to hear that from her father, and you have gone above and beyond. I'm proud to call you Dad, and it's been my greatest honor to be your baby girl.

Christen: Thank you for being the best big sister. You have often fought harder for me than I was willing to fight for myself. Thank you for always including me and making sure I never felt left out even though I didn't have a family of my own. You've been a shoulder to cry on and a friend when I have needed it most. You are so much like mom, and I love that you are a constant reminder of who she was. I love you so much, sister!

Ryan: You're the big brother I've always wanted but never had. Thank you for loving my sister so well and also stepping into the spaces to help take care of me. Sometimes a single girl just needs the help of a big bro, and you have gone above and beyond. You'll never know how much that has meant.

Noni: Thank you for crying both the happy and sad tears with me. You've been willing to walk into the shambles with me and have allowed me to be my true and most messy self. Seeing you so excited about this dream becoming a reality will always be something I will hold close to my heart.

Papa: You really are the best grandfather and truly are one of a kind. I think we all get our sense of humor from you. I know you don't like a big to-do, but I had to say thank you anyway. Your sacrifice and dedication to providing for your family has made all this possible.

Emma Catherine and Bailey: Being your Lolli has been one of my favorite things. The first time I saw you, I knew my whole world would be different and that I would love you forever. You've taught me to laugh and love, and you've been bright lights in my darkest moments. It's my prayer that you will always dream the big and scary dreams and then will chase after them. I'll always be here cheering you on and knowing that God has extraordinary things planned for both of you.

Brenda: Thank you for taking care of my dad so well and being so willing to roll with all the craziness that is our family. You've never tried to replace my mom, but you've been a bonus addition that I'm truly so thankful for. Thank you for loving me as your own and providing so much support and encouragement. When I think of how far we have come since the beginning, I'm always reminded of God's faithfulness.

To my Nashville Life fam: I'm not sure what my life would look like without each of you. You've pushed me and seen me even when I didn't want you to. I've realized not everyone gets to do life in an incredible community, and I feel so blessed that I have you. You all have dared to believe that when God said there would be 12 Months of Spring, He meant it. That has also given me the freedom to believe He had that for me as well. Thank you for never calling me crazy for wanting to write a book and always encouraging me to go for it. I'm not sure what things would look like if I wasn't in a community full of people also chasing their dreams. I've learned it's not just about the church walls, but it's about the people, and each of you feel like home.

To my small-group girls: Thank you for showing up each week and teaching me about true commitment. I needed you guys way more than you will ever need me. I'm so honored to get to do life with each one of you, and I'm so thankful that God saw fit to bring us together. You guys are a huge reason I knew I had to see this thing through. I believe in you and your biggest dreams and want nothing more than all of them to come true. I knew I couldn't ask you to chase your dreams if I wasn't willing to do so myself. I love each of you, and I'm so excited to have a front-row seat to all God is going to do in each of your lives. I will always be your biggest fan and the loudest member of your cheering section.

To all my mommas (Susan, Vicky, Debi, Kathy, Momma Jules, Mom Rowe, Anne, Momma Love, Mayme, Mom Pam, Momma Smith): You are my living and breathing *but God*—proof that God is good and He is faithful and He will stop at nothing to provide for His children. Thank you for stepping into the spaces that felt so empty after I lost my sweet momma. I know many of you promised her you would always look out for me, and you have done that and more. You have championed me, encouraged me, and been quick to remind me how proud my mom would be. Thank you for your prayers, love, and support. I know I'm standing where I am today because you have fought on my behalf time and time again. When I grew weary of lifting up the same prayers, I know each of you were lifting them up for me. I love each of you with my whole heart.

To my small-group leader: Thank you for always cheering me on and encouraging me to chase even my craziest dreams. You embody everything a leader should be, and it means so much that you never gave up on me. Thank you for being so much like Jesus and running to me with arms open wide that day. It will forever be a part of my story and my journey back home. You've always pointed me back to Jesus and never stopped reminding me that He is able. The joy-filled Lauren who learned to dream again is forever grateful.

To the men whom I have cared about or been in love with at some point in my life: I want to thank you too. I found myself trying desperately to protect you, but you are forever going to be such a big part of my story. Without you, I wouldn't be who I am today, and this story wouldn't feel complete. Thank you for the roles you have played and all the lessons learned. I'm grateful for the seasons of life we spent together.

To my future hubby: I don't know who you are or where you are, but in some strange way, I feel like I'm already thankful for you. I've waited a long time to meet you, and I couldn't be more excited for all that is to come. I know a lot of people say this, but I really do believe our marriage will change the world. It will leave a legacy that will point people to Jesus for generations to come. There have been so many times I've been afraid my moment has passed, but I know now more than ever that God's timing is perfect. And He has a special plan for the two of us. I already know you are going to be extra special, because custom made takes a little longer. I can't wait until the day I get to look you in the eyes and acknowledge just how worth it the wait has been. Until we meet . . . know that I'll be praying.

I also want to thank Redemption Press. This book is a very real and very tangible piece of God's redemption in my own life. Thank you for coming alongside of me and helping make this far-off dream become a reality.

And last, but most importantly, thank you to my heavenly Father for the grace I for sure don't deserve but you've extended to me over and over again anyway. Thank you for making sure every bit of the hard was used for good. I know none of it has been wasted.

And thank you for the wait. It's here that I learned to trust you and my faith grew. It was the wait that taught me your goodness and faithfulness wasn't based on me getting everything I wanted. I now know that's just who you are, and that is never going to change. Thank you for being the best kind of Father and making sure I didn't miss out on a fraction of all that you have for me. Your timing is and forever will be perfect.

Introduction

Waiting Well

My feet are on the dashboard of the car, my favorite song is playing on the radio, and we are driving down the most beautiful road—heading into the sunset. My super-handsome hubby reaches over and grabs my hand, and we both smile. There is faint laughter coming from the back seat. The kids are being so cute playing together. I look back at those sweet faces and can't believe they are mine. The day has been so perfect—full of laughter and so much fun.

We are on vacation and have spent the day exploring a city for the first time. There is nowhere else in the world I would rather be or any other people I would rather be with. I am happy and content. And not just the surface happy either. This is the kind of joy you feel deep in your soul. These are the moments I have always dreamed about. This is what I have been waiting for, praying for, and I am so very thankful. I look over at my husband and say, "I can't believe this is our life and that we get to do it all together." He agrees and squeezes my hand a little tighter. This is *the* dream.

I love it in my dreamworld. It's safe and so very comfortable. Everything always turns out just as it should. Sure, a few things might not go according to plan, but before the sun sets that day, the lesson has already been learned and everything turns around. I wipe the fake sweat off my forehead and think, *Phew, I'm glad that's over and everything is back to normal.* My safe, comfortable, and happy life continues to move forward as planned.

These dreamworld stories are what we see on the movie screen. Those are the stories I love to watch, when everything ends just as it should. I want, however, to let you in on a little secret before we go any further.

This isn't one of those stories.

I've pictured this perfect vacation moment so many times, but this dream hasn't become a reality yet. I haven't met my guy, and I am still waiting for my "happily ever after."

I've been told quite often I live in an unrealistic dreamworld. That might be true, but I don't care. That might seem like the most unrealistic thing you have ever heard, but I can't help it. I love dreaming, and I love the they-all-lived-happily-ever-after stories.

I have, however, had to face the harsh reality that life doesn't always turn out the way things do in a fairy tale. As I acknowledge this reality, a groan escapes from somewhere deep in my soul. I'm a dreamer, and no matter how unlikely the fairy-tale outcome is, I simply want to believe everything will come together perfectly in the end.

What happens when the story isn't summed up in one nice, simple telling but drags on through six or seven more books? (Can you say *Harry Potter*?) Maybe God made a promise to you, but you have begun to wonder if He changed His mind. What if there isn't even such a thing as a perfect ending? Or if there is, it looks the opposite of what you planned in your head? What do you do when the ending isn't what you thought it would be?

I have wrestled with similar questions over the last seventeen years, which was right around the time of my first and very dramatic breakup in high school.

I considered waiting to write my story until I'd achieved my perfect ending. I've pictured myself sitting next to my husband and typing out my grand fairy-tale finale. I figured if I waited, I'd really be able to say the ending was worth the wait. When I started writing, I would already have this *ta-da* moment where I could point to my husband and say, "God is faithful."

I haven't, however, had that moment yet. But I have had many profound moments when God has taught me He is still faithful. Even when it's hard, even when I don't fully understand, and even before I get that fairy-tale ending I've always wanted. Yes, even then, He is faithful. There is still pain as I type these words, but I believe God wants me to write from *this* place. This has become such a sacred space. It's not void of frustration, and I still have so many questions. But I believe He wants me to write now, even as I continue to wait.

In the past, I have found deep comfort hearing from someone who is currently walking in similar shoes. There is something so powerful in knowing that the person sharing their story truly understands. When that happens, it becomes clear they aren't just words. They are actually living through what they are saying—not that they once knew what it was like, but they know what it is like *now*.

When we are still hurting and so weary from waiting, we don't want to hear from those on the other side. Or at least I don't.

You should also know I don't feel qualified to write on this topic. I've failed many times over when it comes to waiting—on God's timing, on God's best, on God's plan. I've run ahead of Him so many times.

I've walked away from my writing—this topic—so many times. It's too personal, it hits too close to home, and it hurts too bad. I don't want to write about it. I know I still have so much healing to do and so much more to learn. I still struggle, and I still ache for things to be different.

So how can I write about how to wait well? How could I possibly be of help to other women who feel alone, discouraged, and forgotten? When I still feel all those things too?

Maybe, just maybe, that's why I am supposed to write on this topic.

So here we are, going through this together. Know this: If you have failed horribly at waiting in the past . . . I have too. If some days you really hate being single . . . I do too. If you are sick of waiting . . . I am too. If you are over going to weddings alone . . . I am too. If you are desperate for Jesus to step in and help you through this season . . . I am too.

Even though I have failed and most certainly don't have all the answers, I'm still so hopeful that my sharing will help define a purpose for the waiting. My hope is that somewhere in these pages you will find yourself in my story and that we can go on a journey of healing together. I pray that by sharing all the good and bad of my story we might discover all of this *waiting* was part of God's plan all along. I pray it becomes clear that He is faithful and He is good.

I'm not sure when you first noticed your longing. Or the first time you acknowledged your desire to be married. For me it began in high school. I remember high school being such a fun and hopeful time. The possibilities of what life might become seemed endless. As graduation approached, I felt so optimistic and expectant. Things had always seemed to go according to plan, and I just knew my life after graduation would be more of the same. When my church asked all the seniors to write some of our short-term plans and long-term goals, they were both easy for me.

In the short-term, I would head to Auburn University to live out my dream of playing softball. I had started playing softball when I was six years old, so the goal was always to play softball in college. While most of my classmates spent time with friends or headed to the beach, I spent my summers on softball fields. I wouldn't have traded those summers for anything else though. I knew those moments would be especially worth it once I got to put on the Auburn jersey for the first time.

The long-term goal was also easy for me, and I quote, "To graduate from college and to become the godly wife and mother the Lord wants me to be." These were my words I'd written for our senior program. Being a wife and then a mom was all I ever wanted to do (besides play softball at Auburn). I love that people have lofty career goals and certain things they want to accomplish, but I didn't care about any of that.

They were pretty simple goals, but they were my dream.

I had a plan and had no reason to believe it would turn out any differently. We come up with a great plan, tell the Lord all about that plan, and then said plan just falls into place, right?

My eighteen-year-old self believed that truth with her whole heart.

At first, the plan did seem to be falling into place. I headed to Auburn on a softball scholarship, and all of my dreams would soon come true. College was an amazing time and one I'm so thankful for. Again, this time in college was super busy with all the responsibilities student athletes must take on, but I wouldn't have traded it for the world. Getting to live out my dream of wearing the Auburn jersey was even better than I had imagined.

In my bigger plan, I would meet and then date my husband in college. I would graduate with a degree in elementary education, teach for two years while we enjoyed being married, and then, once we had kids, I would be a stay-at-home mom. It all seemed so very simple to me.

But it didn't happen that way at all. Instead, I fell in love with the wrong guy. For a couple years I thought he would one day be my husband. We had even dreamed and discussed plans for our future together. Unfortunately, he loved multiple women, which didn't end well for any of us.

I walked across the stage at graduation very single and still very much nursing a broken heart from my failed relationship. I decided to stay at Auburn and study for my master's degree, mostly because I didn't know what else to do. I still held out hope that I would meet the right guy as I finished my last year of school. But my master's graduation ceremony came and went as well, and there was still no guy in sight.

I started applying for teaching jobs in multiple cities—something I never thought I'd do without my husband's input. You see, in my plan, my husband and I would decide where we would live together. I never dreamed I would be making decisions on my own.

I eventually picked Nashville since I knew some people there already, and I accepted a teaching job.

I felt excited during this time. There were so many new things in my life, but it still felt like something was missing. The dreamer in me decided that my husband must be waiting for me in Nashville. That idea helped me make peace with the fact that I hadn't met my husband yet. I just knew once I got settled he would make his grand entrance. But that didn't happen either. Years passed, and there was more waiting than I could ever imagine. In fact, I'm currently thirty-five and still waiting.

During those years of waiting, I have had such a love/hate relationship with my singleness. Often, I love being single and the freedom it allows me to enjoy. Without another person to consider, I can travel, stay up as late as I want, or meet up with friends any time I want. I can make my own decisions. I-am-female-hear-me-roar type of stuff. I have also, however, hated being single. I have felt lonely at times, and having to go to things by myself has gotten so very old. Year after year, I have been so hopeful and certain that my hubby stood right around the corner—only to be proven wrong over and over again. I have cried more tears than I can count. I've been angry and bitter. I've wondered why the Lord had forgotten me. I have spent seasons praying for my husband and writing him many letters in hopes that would bring him into my life quicker. I have also had times when I couldn't bear even thinking about him.

Sometimes I wanted to be married so badly I couldn't bring myself to pray for him any longer. I've prayed, begged, pleaded, and even given up the idea completely.

You name it, I've done or felt it.

I've even found myself going through each of these emotions all in one day.

One Saturday, I had just spent most of my day with a couple girls from my small group. I felt so full of love and hope and certainty that on this day I was really living out my purpose. As I processed my feelings with a friend, I realized all my free time was truly a gift. If I had a man in my life, I would be thinking about going on dates and the next time I would spend time with him. Being in a relationship would consume so many of my waking hours, and my free time would be much more limited. But here's the thing: I was grateful for the free time but would have also traded it in a heartbeat. As I continued to process with my friend, I explained that the free time was such a gift, yet it wasn't a gift I asked for or would have chosen. Furthermore, it was a gift I would gladly give back. Thanks, but no thanks. I'm good. I was thankful for the free time, but at the same time, I wished I didn't have it. I was so ready to start sharing my life with someone else.

I share all of that because I want you to know I understand. I've been there. I *am* there. I'm writing to you while I'm standing right in that spot, standing right beside you. My deepest prayer is that my story can bring you comfort as we stand in this spot together.

I want you to understand how God fits into my story. How I still believe in His goodness even when my prayers don't get answered. How even though I'm still waiting, I believe He still has a plan.

If you're like me, you've learned to quantify the waiting. You know, I've waited this long, so I have the most points. I win. My hope is that we strive to no longer do that as we show grace to others and ourselves. There is no points scale here. Instead, I want to look at this season in our lives with fresh eyes and a better understanding. We all have been or will be waiting for something at some point in our lives. The question is, how do we wait *well?*

I've learned life is too messy to come together like a little package with a bow tied on top. There is not always a fairy-tale ending. Waiting well is not accomplished so we can receive that thing we've wanted for so long sooner. Waiting well means letting God accomplish His purpose—to use the wait to learn and grow into the person He longs for us to be. A person more like Him.

This waiting really isn't about the happy ending at all.

Let's Get *Real*

- Sometimes during the waiting you feel like you are thriving and other times you are just surviving. Where are you at right now?
- Are you waiting well? Have you ever considered what it might look like to wait well? I encourage you to grab a journal or your phone and write down your thoughts.

Heavenly Father, I want to wait well but I have no idea what that actually looks like. Can you help me? On my own all I can see is all the dreams that are not being met. Can you show me that you are in this with me? Will you help me see your goodness even now? Use this time to teach me and mold me into who you have created me to be. Thank you for loving me enough to not let me skip a moment of the wait, and thank you for reminding me that no part of this season will be wasted.

Chapter 1

Dealing with Disappointments

Have you ever wanted to give up simply due to an abundance of disappointment in your life? Has it ever seemed too painful to continue to hope that your dreams could come true?

I asked both of these questions often as I walked through my own disappointments. I didn't realize it then, but I've learned that disappointment can ruin us like few other things can. Feeling disappointed caused me to lose all hope and led me to make decisions I never thought I would make.

Remember earlier when I told you my eighteen-year-old self believed everything would work out just the way she wanted it to? In most instances in my life, things *had* usually gone according to my plans. I'd had a couple of horrible relationship experiences, but after I'd worked through the heartbreak, it became clear that God had better things planned for me. When I look back on those times now, I see how everything did work out for the best. God had my best interests at heart—like He always does.

When I lost my mom to cancer in 2013, however, it was hard to find the silver lining. In the initial days, weeks, and months after she passed away, I felt certain no good would ever come from this situation. Losing my mom was extremely difficult and seemed so unfair. My mom's faith had been so strong, and she'd fought so hard to stay here with our family. When most would have said enough was enough, she would agree to the next treatment and the next. She never stopped fighting or believing she would be healed. When all our prayers were not answered how we thought they would be, I became confused. For the first time, I started doubting if God was as good as I had always thought He was.

While my mom was spending her final days on earth, I started dating my best friend. I'm so thankful for that relationship now. He brought such joy and comfort into one of the hardest times of my life. When so much in my life didn't make sense, being with someone I felt so comfortable with made so much sense.

Until it didn't.

After about a year of dating, I began to feel unrest in the relationship. Looking back, I think it was the Holy Spirit prompting me to end things. As most people tend to do, however, I fought those feelings—determined to make the relationship work. For months I pleaded with God to just let me have this one thing. I couldn't imagine letting go of the relationship and dealing with a breakup on top of the grief I was still experiencing. When that didn't work, I tried to manipulate and fix the situation on my own. I knew deep down what I needed to do but wasn't ready to face that reality. I tried to mold my friend into who I thought he needed to be. I thought that maybe if he became that person, the breakup would no longer be necessary. (Side note: I've since learned once you start trying to change the person you are dating, the relationship becomes super unhealthy.) We began to disagree and argue a lot more. Our once-loving, fun relationship became difficult. We no longer enjoyed spending time together. I tried to fix the strain and obtain peace in the relationship again. I wanted it to work so badly. When I couldn't fix the relationship, I realized something had to change.

I could no longer convince myself that staying in the relationship was okay and things could work out. I finally decided to end the relationship, which immediately brought so much peace. Obeying will always do that. It felt like a weight was lifted off my shoulders, but I also felt so much pain and sadness. The peace I felt reassured me I was making the right decision, but this wasn't even close to what I wanted. Even though I ended the relationship, I was still experiencing so much heartbreak.

As time went on, I began to find it extremely difficult to truly let go of my ex. I knew to fully move on, I needed a clean break, which included no communication. In fact, I had even told my ex several times that we could no longer talk. The communication break, however, would only last for a short period before I would get sad and lonely and would reach out to him again. Then the cycle would start all over again. I rationalized these decisions because we weren't officially getting back together. We were just chatting—being friends. But what was going on in my heart was so much deeper than that. Even though I knew we weren't getting back together, my heart still felt so tethered to his.

We went around and around in this unhealthy, circular pattern for almost a full year. Over and over again, we both were continually hurt.

I am not proud of this period of my life. I made a lot of mistakes I hope to never make again. When we are in the middle of making unhealthy decisions, we can't always see the truth. I find it interesting that we always rationalize our behavior with the idea that our situation is different from others. We feel like we're somehow the exception.

Now, I know I was looking to him to fill a void—a void no

human was ever meant to fill. The hurt and pain never needed to last as long as it did. If I would have simply dealt with my sadness and disappointment, things could have looked so much different. Running back to what felt safe and comfortable was so much easier though.

Around the Fourth of July that year, I wanted to be at the beach with him and his family, but since we were no longer a couple, I knew it wasn't a good idea. As I sat on my bed crying one night, I started to wonder if it would really be so bad if I went. I knew it might be harder for me in the long run, but I also knew it would be a fun escape from the sadness. The dialogue in my head told me to do it even if it wasn't the healthiest choice. I was tired of fighting and trying to stay away from the things I wanted to do. I looked up flights and even went as far as reaching out to my ex's mom to say I was thinking about coming.

As I attended church the next day, my mind was still focused on making the trip happen. Even the thought of going to the beach was exciting. I knew it would be so much fun. I honestly can't tell you what the sermon was about that day. But somewhere in the middle of the service, I began to see the situation with a different filter. Instead of just wanting to do what was easiest in the moment, I saw past that to a future that might possibly involve healing from my current heartbreak. Letting Jesus shine a light into our hurts has the power to change our perspective. I decided that day I was not going to run away to the beach. Once again, I felt peace come rushing in after my act of obedience. This moment of clarity did not fix everything, but it was a step in the right direction. In these situations, all we can do is take one step at a time.

I later learned that my ex met a woman that weekend at the beach who would eventually become his wife. I am not saying I did or did not have anything to do with that, but I do know that staying in Nashville that weekend removed me from the equation.

When I learned my ex had a new girlfriend, all the pain and sadness came spilling out. I had epic meltdowns almost daily. I'd known my ex would eventually move on; I just wasn't ready to actually face that reality. I felt like such a mess as all the hurts I had tried to keep hidden rose to the surface. Watching my ex move on made me wonder if God even saw me. Did He even know I was still here, still hurting, and still so very single? When we try to compare our stories to other people's it often leaves us feeling like we are missing out. Even though it might feel small, that kind of shift in focus can be detrimental to how we are viewing our current situation.

It was during this season of disappointment the Enemy saw his opportunity to knock me down. That's what he does. He doesn't play fair or nice. He knows when and where we are most vulnerable.

Lysa TerKeurst explains this so well in her book *It's Not Supposed to Be This Way.*

> The enemy uses disappointments to cause so much trouble in an unsettled heart. A heart hungry for something to ease the ache of disappointment is especially susceptible to the most dangerous forms of desire. Especially when that heart isn't being proactive about taking in truth and staying in community with healthy, humbled people living out that truth.[1]

Man, do I ever know that statement to be true. The Enemy knew right where to attack me—he used my disappointments to grab a foothold. Walking away from truth and everything I had always known to be true about God started with just one seed of doubt. Sometimes one thought is all it takes. I remember thinking, *If God really was good, would so much have been taken away from me?* Losing my mom and my boyfriend—who had been my best friend—felt like God was doing all He could to take things away

[1] Lisa TerKeurst, *It's Not Supposed to Be This Way* (Nashville: Thomas Nelson, 2018).

from me. Where was His goodness in my life? The small seeds of doubt slowly, but surely, started to put down some roots in my heart. As time went on, that small bit of doubt grew into a complete misunderstanding of God and His purpose for my life. I started believing He wasn't the good and loving Father I had always thought Him to be. He had let me down and failed me on so many accounts. Then, I started to wonder if living my life as a Christian was really worth it. What good did it do me? I still felt heartache, despair, and disappointment. I had worked so hard to do the right things and be a good person. Yet I felt like I didn't have much to show for my efforts. I was still lonely, sad, single, and longing for a family that seemed like it might never come.

It's still amazing to me how a little doubt mixed with disappointment can cause such devastation.

What followed was a lot more questions: "Why, God, why? Why couldn't you have just saved my mom? Why did you make me end things with my boyfriend? Why did he have to move on so easily while I continue to hurt and grieve? You must not love me like I thought you did. Do you even see me anymore? Do you know I am still hurting? I have tried so hard to be good, and all I have left is so much disappointment."

If I had simply turned to a friend or loved one during this time, things might not have taken the dark turn they did next. But I let fear and shame keep me quiet. How could I explain to anyone that the girl who had spent her whole life in church wasn't even sure God was good anymore? I felt like I should be joyful because there was so much good in my life. I actually had everything I needed, and I knew there were so many people that had it so much worse than me. The shame kept telling me there should be peace and there should be joy because I've always said God had a plan for me. But I certainly wasn't feeling any joy. And there was way too much shame to actually be honest with anyone, so I kept it all to myself. Now, I know these thoughts were exactly what the Enemy wanted me to think. He wanted me to keep quiet, and he wanted me to believe no one would understand. If he can isolate us, he can influence us. With me, he did just that.

Pretty soon, I stopped talking to God altogether. This didn't happen all at once, but over time I prayed less and less until prayer was no longer a part of my life at all anymore. I just didn't see the point in keeping up a relationship that had been so hurtful. I was afraid if I stopped showing up places, people would realize something was going on, and they might start asking me questions. In order to avoid this, I kept up most of my normal routines of going to church and small group and being around friends. But I kept everyone at arm's length. I knew all the right things to say at small group, and I let people in just enough so they would leave me alone. I hoped those around me wouldn't ask too many questions. If they did, I might not be able to keep it together. I was convinced there was no way I could explain what was really going on in my heart.

I began to feel so lost, and things became really dark. Bitterness and anger intensified my loneliness. Somewhere along the way, I just stopped trusting the Lord completely. My life looked like such a mess. I had always believed God had a future for me, and that had brought hope. But now I couldn't see any of it. Nothing looked hopeful. I felt so bad for feeling this way, but I didn't seem to be able to change it. I also really wanted to be happy for those around me experiencing such great life changes. I wanted to be excited for those people getting engaged or getting married or having a baby. But I just wasn't. Which brought more shame.

As the holidays approached that year, I decided I needed to push all of the hurt and sadness aside. I made the decision to just enjoy the holidays, enjoy being with my family, and try to have fun. I would deal with the shambles of my life in January.

Once the holidays were over and the new year began, I quickly realized I still felt no different. I really thought a brand-new year would bring new excitement and a new sense of purpose, but nothing had changed. This harsh reality hit me hard.

As I tried to get back into my routines, I woke up feeling odd and not like myself at all. I began to wonder if this was what depression felt like. I had never experienced feeling depressed but was afraid this might be it. I was able to go through the motions of the day but felt like I was in a fog. This new feeling scared me. As that week went on, I found myself wanting to stay in bed more and more. This was not normal for me, and I had no idea what to do about it. I felt weak and like something was very wrong with me, which brought a lot of embarrassment. I didn't want anyone to know what was going on.

Eventually this worsening depression felt like a heavy burden, and it was too heavy for me to bear. I had put so much hope in the fact that things would feel different when January hit. Now, I felt like my only option was to go into self-preservation mode and try to survive any way I could. Instead of thinking about what I would do on any given day, I would wonder how I could *survive* another day.

Depression is never an instant thing. I didn't just wake up one morning depressed. My journey into depression was a prolonged period of no longer being willing or even being able to feel my emotions. It was so painful to feel all the sadness and hurt day after day. Eventually the darkness and despair became like a friend to me, and I began to sit in those emotions. I knew praying and reading the Bible could be helpful, but they felt like the last things I wanted to do. I learned to push my feelings down deeper in an attempt to avoid them. And I latched on to anything that would provide an escape and help me feel a little better.

When we fight to escape our own feelings, we seek ways to numb the pain. Some people turn to drugs, alcohol, or other substances. But whatever we are using to numb the pain is harmful to us. We often rationalize and justify ourselves with the idea that what we are doing isn't as bad as someone else's efforts to numb their pain. If the things we turn to aren't sex, drugs, or other illegal things, then we think we are good. My ridiculously long daily naps and endless hours spent on Netflix, however, were just as damaging to my heart. Even the best things not in their proper place can become a hindrance to our living our healthiest and best selves.

Your emotions might tell you all kinds of things that feel so true in that moment, but most of them are lies. Thinking no one will understand you, therefore "you need to keep quiet" is a lie. Thinking you are stuck in this place of pain, hurt, and depression is a lie. Thinking whatever you have done is too bad for God to forgive you is a lie. The Enemy wants you to feel trapped where you are right now, but you aren't. You never have been, and you never will be, because Jesus already paid the penalty for our sins on the cross. I didn't fully understand this truth, but after walking through this difficult season, I do now. I believe this is why the Bible says to "be transformed by the renewing of your mind" (Romans 12:2). Our emotions can pull us in so many different directions, so we must get intentional about renewing our minds and returning to truth. And that real truth can only be found in the Bible.

These lessons are a part of the goodness that can come from the difficult and hard seasons we walk through. We learn way more about who God is during the hard times than we do when everything is going according to plan. Fruit grows in the valleys and not on the mountaintops.

During my season of depression, I had moments when I fought and really tried to pull myself out of the pit. In those moments, I let some people in but not fully. I was scared to let someone see my whole mess. What would my mess say about me? What would it indicate about my faith? I let people in, but only into the shallow parts of myself. I went back to counseling, too, but still wasn't fully honest and transparent with my therapist. Unfortunately, just showing up to counseling wasn't enough. I needed to actually tell the truth before any real healing could take place. I was simply putting Band-Aids on top of the hurt. They helped stop the bleeding for a little while but never helped me get to the root of the issues. When I'd make no progress, the fight no longer seemed worth it, and I would give up again.

Life looked so different than I thought it would by this point. I was thirty and still single, which was never a part of the plan. My mom was gone. I thought I'd have so much more time with her. And my dream of being a mom seemed so far away—perhaps even impossible. Even my attempt to buy a house had fallen through. I was nowhere near where I'd wanted to be by this time in my life.

The Enemy loves to make us think things couldn't possibly get worse and that no one else has come close to experiencing all the difficulties we've had. As we focus on our problems, they become bigger and bigger, and soon we aren't able to see anything else.

After ending things with my ex, I felt like I had earned a reward for doing the right thing. God asked me to end the relationship and I did, so a reward should follow. Of course, I thought I knew exactly what that reward should look like. I had it all planned out in my head, and I had imagined the moment many times. It would involve looking into the handsome face of the man who would be my husband. Then, I would know all the pain and heartache had been worth it. Then, I would really be able to talk about how good God is.

But the reward never came, and my disappointments grew.

When your hope is tied to things working out perfectly—in *your* way—you start to make compromises. You start to initiate your own plans. Since God wasn't going to give me the thing I so desperately wanted, I would take matters into my own hands. It seems kind of silly now, but back then, I believed that's exactly what I had to do. At first, it felt freeing. I could do what I wanted, when I wanted. Making the right choice had often felt like a prison sentence. I didn't understand back then that God was not trying to be cruel, but He was only trying to protect me. The Enemy wants us to believe we are somehow missing out when we follow Jesus, and he uses this lie to sink us deeper into our own darkness.

We should never be surprised when the temptation to go our own way shows up during a moment of weakness. The Enemy is no fool. He knows he has already been defeated, so he must use schemes and tricks to manipulate us. A long time ago, I heard a pastor say, "The only power the Enemy has is the power of the lie." This became so true in my own life. He came and whispered lies that included things like: *If God really loved you, He would have already given you the husband you have always dreamed of. Making your own choices will be so freeing and so much fun.* Once the Enemy starts to fill our heads with lies, we must decide if we'll believe those lies.

I felt so justified in my feelings that I absolutely took the bait.

Sin always looks enticing. After all, if we saw the destruction sin would do and the death it would bring, we would always say no. Instead, we always think we are an exception to the rule. We always think we can handle anything life (and the Enemy) throws our way.

That just isn't true. Never has been and never will be.

We see this in the life of David. In 2 Samuel 11, we see that David's fall into sin all started with a single, lingering glance at a beautiful woman. I can't put words into his mouth, but I imagine he believed he would be able to handle a single glance. Then, when he sent for Bathsheba, I can only guess that he believed no harm could come from this action. That is always what the Enemy wants us to believe. But for David, the single glance turned into a series of sins, which caused devastation to a lot of lives.

I have seen that same scenario play out in my own life. Once a new guy entered the picture, I believed I could handle it on my own. He was a really nice guy who was already a friend. I believed I would have no problem keeping him in the friend zone. From the very beginning, he asked the hard questions and gave me a place to share without any judgments. It felt good to have someone so interested in me and giving me so much attention. But here's the thing: this guy wasn't a Christian. Therefore, I knew, deep down, a relationship with him was wrong. I had been told over and over at church it was wrong, but I also know from past experiences choosing to date someone who didn't share my beliefs wasn't a good idea. I had been down that road before, and I knew it would only lead to heartbreak. I rationalized the whole thing, however, by deciding we could only be friends. If we were just friends, it would all be okay.

When this man and I first started talking, my church was starting twenty-one days of the Daniel Fast. I didn't feel like I was in the kind of headspace necessary for a fast, but I decided I would go along with what my church was doing. I don't really know the reason I didn't completely walk away from my church community during this time, but I'm thankful I didn't. Staying bound to my church eventually would be so vital to my healing.

A couple of days before we started the fast, a friend came over so we could cook a good "last" meal and enjoy each other's company. I had gotten so good at putting on a happy face. It didn't even feel like an act anymore. By the end of the night, however, she said, "Is everything okay? I just feel like you are really sad." Cue the tears. I couldn't hold it in any longer. She saw me. I was no longer able to hide. She let me cry, and then she prayed for me. I woke the next day feeling like I had gained a little strength back. For the first time in a long time, I felt a small amount of hope. I was ready to fight again.

I decided I would obtain some victory during this fast. I would start to take my life back. This would be my redemption season, but it would involve taking some steps forward, even if they felt exhausting. I also decided I would make videos of myself for each day of the fast—a kind of journaling. I would talk about what happened that day and what message God had for me. I had started doing this type of journaling years before, and it had been very powerful, but a full year had passed since I had recorded myself, which was very telling of the season I had been in. I believed, however, this would be a defining moment in my healing, so I wanted to document it. I wanted to be able to look back at the videos and remember God's faithfulness. Now I'm so thankful I have these videos but for a much different reason.

To really maximize the fast, I also decided I would give up watching TV. Now, watching TV isn't necessarily bad, but I had begun using it to avoid feeling sad. When alone in bed at night, everything always seemed so dark and lonely. I knew using Netflix as a crutch was not helping me resolve my issues, so I tried to stop the habit. I tried very hard to cut out anything that would prolong my healing. The sheer fact I felt like fighting again brought a sense of relief. Maybe everything wasn't as bad as I thought it was, and I could pull myself out of this season of despair.

On day two of the fast, I began to notice the repeated patterns in my life, like when I had continued to talk with my ex in the past. Although it felt so good to have someone to talk to, I realized talking to this new guy was only filling the voids in a new way. Talking to him on the phone at night for hours before bed gave me something new and exciting to focus on but was also just replacing what I had given up—Netflix. In my life, I had often reverted to this pattern. I had so often turned to men to help satisfy and meet some need I felt inside. I didn't know how to simply be with myself, my thoughts, and my feelings. I needed to fill up that space with *something*.

I knew I could no longer be so passive if I wanted things to change. Without giving myself time to change my mind, I called my friend and let him know I could no longer continue talking to him like we'd been doing. I knew I didn't have all the answers, but I also knew I couldn't walk down the same path and expect a different result. My friend took it all very well. He said he understood and would respect my decision. This victory felt really good!

I wish I could tell you that I continued along that path and things started to turn around, but that isn't even close to the truth.

As the fast continued, my feelings began to shift, like they often do. When the fast started, I was so expectant. But then as the days dragged on, old thought patterns began to resurface. My decision to make changes didn't magically transform my old thought patterns or stop the Enemy from attacking. The thoughts that crept into my mind were things like: *It really won't be that bad if you just talk to him every now and then. You know, like twice a week. You guys are just friends, so there really won't be any harm in talking to a friend. It feels good to have someone concerned about you, so there can't really be anything wrong with it. You are strong enough to protect your heart.*

We began speaking again. In the beginning, we only talked a couple times a week, but that eventually turned into texting all day and then hours spent on the phone every night. Again, talking on the phone to someone isn't bad, but there was such a deeper issue there for me. It was much more than just an innocent phone call. I knew this guy wasn't right for me, so deep down, I knew it wasn't a good situation for me to be in.

As Lysa TerKeurst said, sin "promises to fill the gaps of disappointments with satisfaction. In reality it goes straight to our hearts and fills them with shame."[2] Seeking this satisfaction starts as one little action that we believe won't be a big deal, and it takes us somewhere we never thought we would go. This was absolutely the case for me.

The long conversations with my friend continued. I continued to lie to myself and others around me. I had always maintained that we were just friends, but there was something much deeper going on. Come summertime, I basically ran away with him on an adventure out west. At this point, people close to me started to pick up on the fact that something was very wrong. These people reached out to me and asked me the hard questions. But I either ignored them or lied straight to their face.

If you find yourself avoiding being honest about something or irritated by people who are trying to be kind and loving to you, it's probably because something is off. When we keep things in the dark, it provides the illusion that things are better than they really

[2] TerKeurst, *It's Not Supposed to Be This Way.*

42

are. Bringing things to the light lets us see a clearer picture of the actual reality and not just the reality we have created in our minds.

This is exactly why I like exercising in dim lighting. When the lights aren't bright, there are all kinds of shadows, and there is this illusion that my muscles are way more defined than they actually are. I know this is very vain of me, but it's also very true. The second I turn on more lights, however, everything looks different. Instead of, *Oh man, I really have abs!*, it's, *I really should do a lot more sit-ups.* I can see everything so much clearer in the light.

The same thing happens when we put on makeup in the dark. I'm not sure if you have ever done this before. But we can feel so good about how great we look only to get in our car, look in the mirror, and find we have mascara everywhere. No wonder we love keeping things in the dark. The light can feel harsh, but it's so helpful. Bring things to the light, and let at least one person speak truth to you. Sometimes even telling just one person can change the way you view a situation. Often you begin to see things through their perspective instead of just the false reality you've created in your mind. I really wish I had let at least one person into my situation. It would have been very beneficial.

On our trip out west, things became physical for the first time. Truth be told, before we got physical, we were already more than just friends. But in my mind, if we hadn't physically crossed a line, I could still easily represent to myself and those around me that we were just friends. Right before he went to kiss me for the first time, I realized I had a choice to make. I remember thinking, *I've tried to do the right things for so long, and I still haven't gotten what I want. It's time to do what I want to do without worrying about what I think I am supposed to do.*

The next morning, I felt so much shame and was embarrassed I had let things go too far. At lunch that day, I let him know that could never happen again. It had been a one-time-only thing. I think, however, we both knew that wasn't true, and it wasn't long before things got physical again.

This is what sin does: it creeps in, bringing death and destruction in its path.

For the next year, I did whatever I wanted whenever I wanted. I made poor choice after poor choice. I lied to those closest to me and then made up more lies to cover up those lies. I started playing house with this man and doing things I had promised myself and God I would wait until marriage to do. I did way more sexually than I ever had before. When I started feeling guilty, I simply drank more to ignore the obvious. And I pushed away the people who loved me the most.

Within a year, I went from being "just friends, it's no big deal if I talk to him on the phone" to playing house and ruining so many of the good things in my life.

All because of my disappointment in how I thought life should play out. All because I was trying to fill a void.

The Lord has always said He had plans for me (Jeremiah 29:11), but I got tired of waiting for those plans to come to fruition. Disappointment can be such a gift to point us back to our Savior, or it can be the birthplace of doubt, leading us to believe God is not actually the good God we think He is.

I'm so thankful my story didn't end here. Despite all my bad decisions, I was about to learn God still had a plan.

Let's Get *Real*

- Have disappointments ever led you to do something you wouldn't normally do?
- Is there an area of your life you are currently experiencing disappointment now?
- Is there anything that you are trying to hide in the dark that you need to be honest with someone about?

God, I have so much shame (or whatever you are feeling) admitting this, but I believe you are a safe place I can always go. So here I am bringing you my true and honest self. I feel so disappointed and let down by the way things have turned out. I want to believe you are a good and loving Father, but I am just not sure I can see it right now. Can you show me your goodness? Will you remind me you are still faithful even while I am still waiting? I know I can't continue to walk this road by myself—it hurts too badly. I need you to step in. Will you also show me one person in my life I can be honest with? I know I am going to need some encouragement and accountability during this season. I believe this season can be different, but I need your help to overcome my doubt. Thank you for loving me so perfectly, despite all my mistakes. I want to see your goodness now, even before I get that thing I've always wanted.

Chapter 2

I Am with You Always!

What do we do if we have already messed up and have taken things into our own hands? I say this next part with tenderness and love, because I know what I'm about to say is far from easy.

Once we have messed up, we must do the only thing and go to the only person that will ever make it better. We must repent and run to Jesus. We give Him the hurt, the fears, and all the pain. If we put our trust in Him, He can turn all of our pain into something beautiful. We must make a conscious decision to say, "God, I can no longer hold this. I need you to take it."

I remember the moment so clearly when I *finally* reached the end of myself.

Up until this point in my life, I had always been "churched" just a little too much. I'm so thankful my parents chose to make being in a body of believers an important part of our week, but an unintended result of that was I always felt kind of *comfortable* in my faith. I knew right from wrong. I knew what to do and what not to do. I had it all together. Or so I thought.

Disappointments led me down a very dark path. Along that path, I learned the hard truth that we are all just a couple of bad decisions away from turning into a complete mess. If I'd had it all together, I wouldn't have needed someone to come rescue me— which is what Jesus does for all of us. My years in church didn't make me an exception to the rule . . . all have sinned and fall short of the glory of God (Romans 3:23). I am human. Therefore, I am needy. I have messed up. I have sinned and am in need of God's grace.

After what we will call "my season of wandering," for the first time, I was able to really relate and identify with the prodigal son. In Luke 15 of the Bible, Jesus tells the story of a son who decides he no longer wants to wait until his father passes to receive his inheritance. He wants what's due to him now. The father grants his request, and the son decides to leave and eventually blows through all the money. I often read stories like this in the Bible and think, *How could he ever do that? Didn't he know it would be better if he waited to get his money? Geez, he has zero patience.*

Then I take a step back and realize I can see so much of myself in this story. I don't want to wait. I want what I want when I want it. I, too, have lost sight of the big picture and made decisions based on what felt most enjoyable in the moment. The son didn't want to wait for his money and decided to spend it however he wanted without thinking about any of the consequences. Each time I decide my plans are better than God's, I become exactly like this son. Each time I get tired of waiting and decide to take things into my own hands, my decisions are just like the decisions of this son whom I am so quick to judge.

I'd always had my life together enough to never consider myself a prodigal daughter. I hadn't strayed. I didn't need to "return." But the more I thought about my current situation, the more I realized I needed to return to my heavenly Father. I *had* strayed, and just like the prodigal son, I, too, was far from home.

I saw, for the first time ever, my need and lack. I felt like I had messed up so badly I wasn't sure if God was even willing to help me anymore. My incorrect view of God was that He was just waiting for me to return to Him so He could punish me. I deserved it after all.

Nothing could have been further from the truth. But in those moments of darkness and despair, my shame told me I deserved to be punished.

Somehow in the middle of all the anger, darkness, pain, and bad decisions, Jesus still came for me. I didn't have myself "together" yet, and I hadn't stopped making the bad decisions, but that didn't seem to matter. God still stepped into my situation and shined light into the dark corners of my heart.

I first noticed God shining light into my life in February of 2017, when I attended a relationship and marriage conference my church hosted. At the end of the first day, I sat in a room surrounded by other singles. Before the session started, I had already become annoyed thinking about what I might hear. I had heard so many ideas of what my singleness should look like, and I had started tuning most of it out. I was tired of married women telling me being single was such a gift and to just enjoy my singleness. When these conversations started, I fought hard not to roll my eyes. As you can imagine, more of the same teaching was the last thing I wanted to hear.

But then something refreshing happened. The woman who got up to speak was married but had gotten married at thirty-seven. She didn't try to sugarcoat the hard in the waiting. She talked so openly and freely about how hard it had been for her. Her honesty was refreshing. I really liked knowing I wasn't alone in the hard and that someone else understood what it had been like all these years. She really understood me. In that moment, I decided to lean in to what she was saying and also to what God might want to say to me through her.

At the end of her talk, she asked for anyone that needed prayer to come forward. I needed prayer very badly, and I really wanted this woman to pray over me. But I was afraid people might be watching and might be wondering why I needed prayer. I was desperate, however, for things to change, so I went anyway. Nothing super crazy or out of the ordinary happened as I stood nervously in the front of that room. But I did pray a brief prayer to invite God into my situation.

It went a little something like this: *I have no idea if I have already messed this whole thing up too badly. But if my childhood dream of the godly husband and the marriage that points people to you is still possible, I still want that. Will you help me?*

I didn't suddenly feel totally different, and my circumstances didn't immediately change. But that decision still played a big part in my total healing. God longs to be invited into any and all situations in our life. He doesn't care what we have done; He just wants our true and honest hearts. That day I let my walls down and let Him all the way in.

A month after I prayed that prayer, I was invited to an event at a friend's house where a woman named Donna led the event. What I didn't know then was this woman would eventually become my counselor. As she shared some of her own story that night, around the room tears began flowing. She told us that during a hard season in her life, she had asked God some of the very same questions I had been thinking. She put words to things I hadn't been brave enough to say out loud. Her honesty inspired me, and her words were a healing balm my soul desperately needed.

After the event concluded, I went up to her with tears spilling out of my eyes and down my cheeks and asked if I could come to her office to talk to her more. Looking back now, I see how God was taking care of me even when I wasn't ready to take care of myself. The seemingly small and insignificant detail of being invited to a friend's house ended up having a lasting effect on me.

Did you see the pattern? These women were brave enough to be truly vulnerable and honest about their struggles, and it unlocked something in me. I felt less alone, less crazy, and a whole lot less afraid to be honest. Vulnerability is the key to setting people free.

Week after week I sat on Donna's comfy couch and cried and cried and then cried some more. I finally voiced all my questions and my fears. Once I started telling the truth, it was hard to stop the steady stream of hurts and disappointments that had been tucked away so deeply for so long. I shared with her my fears about God. I told her about the secret relationship I was in. She exuded love and understanding. She didn't tell me I was stupid for being in this relationship, which is what I expected to hear from people. She didn't tell me I needed to end things. She simply listened and lovingly pointed me to Jesus.

One day she explained to me that what I was saying I wanted and what I was actually doing were competing with each other. I wanted to marry someone who shared my faith, and I had begun to believe that was still possible for me. At the same time, however, I was still engaging in this secret relationship with a man who wasn't a Christian. This back-and-forth, or up and down, felt like a roller coaster—leaving me in a constant state of turmoil. She then said something really simple but also really profound: "It's up to you when and if you get off the roller coaster. That is something you get to decide." She advised me to take the next week to think about what it would look like if I got off the roller coaster.

This was one of my healthiest times of processing. Normally, I would jump into decisions without thinking it through. In the past, doing so had left me confused. I often changed my mind over and over again. Or as Donna had said, I was getting on and off the roller coaster over and over again. Doing as she suggested allowed me the time and space to think about what I wanted and decide for myself, not because someone else was telling me to, but because I had thought it through.

At the end of that week, I concluded it was time to get off the roller coaster. Donna and I talked that next week about how I could accomplish this goal, and she helped me process further what doing so would look like. I began to feel a deep peace . . . but I also knew a tough conversation needed to be had.

I needed to call the man I had been secretly dating and tell him I had to end things. In fact, it would be best if we no longer communicated. I knew from my last breakup that my heart couldn't handle another back-and-forth situation. It wouldn't be fair to either of us. I was sure about my decision, and I needed to stick with it.

That conversation scared me. To confront him and to think about what my life would look like without him—it was frightening. I had pushed away so many people trying to keep the relationship hidden. He was really the only one who knew everything going on in my life. How could I tell him I no longer wanted to talk to him at all? It felt like a pretty hopeless situation. When we get desperate enough for change, however, we will do just about anything to make it happen.

On May 17, I went out onto my porch to make the call, afraid of what might come next. I'll never forget how helpless I felt in that moment, knowing what was to come. At that point, I did the only thing that made sense . . . I got on my knees and prayed. I told God I couldn't possibly do this on my own, and I needed His help. There was no way I would survive this phone call or the weeks that were to follow without Him. We often try so hard to keep it together and handle everything on our own, so we can show the world how strong we are. But I could no longer keep it together, and the letting go freed me.

I finally understood that God never needed me to have it all together or to do everything right. He doesn't expect perfection. He just simply longs to be invited in.

When I asked God to step in, the craziest thing happened. God didn't say any of the things I expected Him to. He didn't say, "I'm sorry, but you have created this mess, so I can't do anything about it." He didn't say, "Maybe you should just stay here in your pain a little bit longer, so you really know how badly you have messed up." And He didn't say, "You've actually messed up a lot. We need to have a chat." I felt like I had absolutely earned every one of those chats. You know, the ones where the parent hangs their head and points their finger at you. As I sat there on my knees, however, I didn't hear any of those things.

But what He did whisper straight to my heart that day was, "I am with you always."

That realization changed everything. If God would be with me, then I could make this phone call. And if always really meant *always*, I could face the weeks and months ahead. And if He was with me, I could face going to bed alone that night too.

I won't try to glamorize what came next. That conversation and the time afterward was awful. I couldn't eat (which never happens to me), sleep was sparse, and I felt worse than I had before. I already felt like I was barely keeping it together, and then I decided to throw a breakup into the mix. I thought I had already been at my lowest, but I found another level down.

I think sometimes it can be so confusing when we start taking steps toward healing and things get even worse. We expect to feel better, so it can be very disheartening when we don't. This is another season in which we are very vulnerable. We start to question our decisions, and the Enemy whispers lies about the hard choice not being worth the hard consequences. He convinces us where we just came from wasn't all that bad, and we forget how awful it really was. When I look back, I see the rock bottom was exactly where I needed to be. It was there I learned when God said He would be with me always, He meant it. And rock bottom was where I learned I couldn't do enough or be enough to make myself better, which was such a pivotal lesson, because I was never meant to do it alone.

From there, I started to take small steps forward. I started to tell the truth even though I felt fearful of how the honesty would be received. Each time I opened up to someone, however, I was surprised by how free I felt. People were so kind and gracious to me and were way nicer than I deserved. Even those I had point-blank lied to were willing to forgive me. Then the craziest thing happened. Over time, I watched the Lord redeem all those broken relationships, to the point where friendships are now better and stronger than before. I feel closer and more seen by each of these friends. Only Jesus can do something like that. He takes what the Enemy has meant for harm and uses it all for good.

Telling the truth felt good, but there was one conversation I was still not looking forward to. I still needed to tell my small-group leader. She was a mentor of sorts for me, and she was also a friend. While I was wandering around out west, she had reached out to me countless times, but I ignored every one of those phone calls. Deep down I knew what I was doing was wrong, so I didn't want to hear anything she had to say. Her heart was one of care and concern for me, but I couldn't see that. Instead, I pushed her away over and over again and lied to her many times. Even when I wanted nothing to do with her, however, she still did everything she could to be there for me and love me through it. I had been meeting with her once a month since she was my leader and the person I could go to if I needed anything, yet I still hadn't been brave enough to tell her what was really going on. I knew how to give all the "church answers," so I told her just enough to keep her from asking too many questions. I had treated her so badly, and I felt horrible.

Why do we work so hard to cover up the truth?

The shame we feel or are afraid we might feel keeps us silent. We make up stories in our heads of what might happen if we let someone in. As we keep telling ourselves these lies, the stories become so real and lifelike that we start to believe them as truth. In this case, I thought my small-group leader would be disappointed in me. She knew I knew better than to act the way I'd been acting. She knew I was smart enough to have avoided this. I had sat through enough church services to know what I was doing was wrong.

One fateful day I decided I would be brave, and I would tell her. If I didn't plan it, I would chicken out, and it wouldn't happen. I got to the meeting a little early and was already sweating. The Enemy tried to convince me that day wasn't the best day to tell the truth. I could just tell her later. Then I realized that was the fear talking. In those moments we always have a choice. I could tell her the truth anyway, or I could let the fear stop me. I had to remind myself of the good that had already come from telling the whole truth to others, which helped me realize telling the truth was worth the risk.

When my phone rang, I hoped she was calling to cancel. No such luck. She was simply running late and wanted to go ahead and start talking on the phone while she was on the way there. Before I could talk myself out of telling her what had really been going on, I took a deep breath and said, "I have to tell you something." Then everything came spilling out. I didn't want to leave anything out. If I was going to do this thing, I was going to do it all the way. No more one-foot-in-and-one-foot-out mess. I had seen where that had taken me, and I was done with that.

As I finished telling her everything, I saw her car pull into the parking lot. She didn't say any of the things I thought she would. Instead, she got out of her car and ran to me with her arms wide open. She wrapped me up in the biggest hug and whispered, "I'm so proud of you." I melted. She was so much like Jesus in that moment. For a girl who was still trying to decide whether God was good or not, her actions had a profound and lasting impact on me.

That, my friends, is the character of God. That is His heart for us. He doesn't care that we have lied for years. He doesn't care that we created a terrible mess with our awful choices. He doesn't care about any of that. He simply wants us to come to Him. When we do, He comes running with open arms—just like the father of the prodigal son did and just like my leader did for me.

The Bible says, "If we confess our sins, he is faithful and just and will forgive us our sins and purify us from all unrighteousness" (1 John 1:9). He did that for me, and He will do that for you. That is who God is. That is His heart for us.

I used to hate the idea of repentance. I only understood it as a designated time to feel bad about our mistakes. I don't think there is one person who likes looking back at all the ways they have gotten it wrong or messed up. Repentance, however, is so much more than just feeling bad or guilty about your mistakes. God isn't being cruel when He asks us to repent. He wants us to repent, so we can receive His grace, mercy, and kindness. He knows what's best for us. He knows that our sins (or mistakes) create separation from Him, and repentance is His beautiful plan to close that gap. He knows that when we are in close quarters with Him, we are able to live our freest lives. That is when we are safest, when we are unashamed, and when we understand who we truly are. God wants that for us more than we will ever understand, and He knows the road to that place is through repentance. It's not about always getting it right, but always being willing to admit our mistakes and turn a new way. Repentance is simply this: admitting our mistakes and being willing to make a different decision.

I have often believed this road of surrender and repentance was a road to *less*, but it's actually the road to *success*. The road leads to abundantly more than I could ask for or imagine. I'm so afraid to give up control, but *exceedingly and abundantly more* means God has the absolute best plans for me. I can let go. I can trust that He knows and wants what is best for me.

Maybe you are like me, and this all sounds great, but you are thinking you have already messed up too much. Or maybe you feel like you have already failed this waiting thing, so why even bother?

But those are just lies that you no longer have to believe.

I know it's hard. I know it's scary. But you can let go.

The part I have found most comforting is that I will never have to do any of it on my own. God's forever promise to us is that He is with us always. Not just some of the time, and not when we have gotten it all right, but *always*. There will be situations that come up that are hard, and the waiting will never be easy, but you will never have to handle all of those hard things on your own.

You are not alone. You never have been. You never will be.

You do, however, always have a choice. God never forces us to pick Him, and He never makes us repent. You get to decide if and when you do that. Again, He invites us to make those decisions, because He knows it will be good for us. But the choice is always ours.

We also get to decide if we are going to believe what the Bible says and take God at His word or follow our own feelings. I don't know about you, but my emotions are constantly changing. Therefore, I need an anchor when the winds of disappointment swirl around me and when I just don't feel like I can wait a second longer. I often forget and I often get it wrong, but I can always come back and decide to believe truth over my circumstances. The Bible says about twenty-one times (depending on the translation) that God is with us. I'm no Bible scholar, but it seems to me if He said it that many times, He means it. That is His promise to you, which means no matter what your feelings say or what your circumstances look like, you can cling to that truth. It's not sometimes, it's *always*.

I am with you always, to the very end of the age.
(Matthew 28:20)

Let's Get *Real*

- In what ways do you find yourself relating to the prodigal son?
- Is there anything in your life that is currently making you feel separated from God?
- What do you think God would say to you if you let all of your walls down?
- Do you really believe He has never left you?

Father, I feel so much like the prodigal son right now. I have traded in the best thing for things that will only temporarily satisfy. I have gone my own way, and I feel separated from you. But I know it's time for me to come home. I'm afraid of what you might say to me or how you might respond, but will you help me understand the way you unconditionally love me? Show me what I need to repent of, and show me the way home. I can no longer do it on my own. Will you show me that you are with me always? Thank you for loving me through all of my mistakes and sending your son so I no longer have to feel separated from you.

Chapter 3

The Wait Is in Your Favor

I

s there a purpose for the waiting? Could there possibly be any good that comes from waiting? Does God even remember I'm still waiting? I've asked these questions over and over again. I've sometimes found hope in the answers. I've sometimes heard no answers. I've often cried many tears as I've asked them. And I've also stopped asking them for long periods of time, because even thinking them was too painful. When I look back, however, I can see the little hints of encouragement along the way.

One of these encouraging experiences occurred when my roommate suggested I listen to a sermon she had stumbled upon. She knows me so well and knows I love the big *but God* moments—when all hope seems lost and the situation looks impossible but then God steps in. It's in those moments things make a whole lot more sense. We get a glimpse into how God had been working everything out in the background all along.

While listening to the sermon, I quickly realized the speaker's testimony was full of those moments. Afterward, I had to explain to my coworkers that no one was dying; I just sob when I'm deeply touched. I should have known better than to listen at work.

The speaker was an Australian musician named Mia Fields. I've never met her, but I want to be her friend. As I listened to her testimony, I felt such relief. She hadn't gotten married until later in life, and she knew what it meant to wait. As she spoke, I was again reminded I wasn't the only one who had a deep desire to be married. I wasn't crazy after all. She really understood how hard it was to wait for your husband. She understood *me.* Mia's love story with her husband was such a picture of God's goodness.

To be clear, God is good even before we get what we want, but sometimes He really shows off. When we see all the details He puts into the perfect place, there is no explanation other than God.

In Mia's life, things still didn't look exactly the way she expected them to, and circumstances didn't happen in the timeline she expected. But when she put her faith in God and believed He would answer her prayers for a husband—He delivered in a big way.

One of my favorite parts of her talk was a story about a moment she had with Jesus. She saw herself in a furniture store, and Jesus was pointing out all the good things there. She could pick whatever she wanted. As Mia looked around, though, none of the pieces of furniture seemed to fit her perfectly. As she explained that to Jesus, He told her He could make a custom piece of furniture for her, but she needed to know that *custom made takes longer.* The best things take more time. They just do. Mia decided she was willing to wait on the custom made husband and love story. The details of her story are insane even down to the fact that her husband was gifted a custom made suit to wear at the wedding.

Mia's story has given so much purpose and understanding to my own season of waiting. I want the absolute best even if that means I will have to wait a little longer. I have often reminded myself of this story when I need a little extra encouragement. On the days I don't think I can wait a second longer, I think of all the ways that God is purposefully and carefully working in the background to create my own custom story.

I've found that certain days are just harder for me—there is no set formula. I remember one day I was having an especially hard time waiting for God's plan, and I "stumbled" upon a Scripture passage from Romans 8. When we are willing to open God's Word, what we find there is never an accident. I had read the passage many times, but now, during this season of waiting, it resonated with me more.

> That is why waiting does not diminish us, any more than waiting diminishes a pregnant mother. We are enlarged in the waiting. We, of course, don't see what is enlarging us. But the longer we wait, the larger we become, and the more joyful our expectancy. (Romans 8:24–25 MSG)

This image from Romans is so beautiful to me and makes so much sense. I understand waiting is good and helpful for a pregnant mother, so why would my wait be any different? How amazing is God to make sure "we are enlarged in the waiting" (v. 24)? There is purpose. When we wait, we're not simply sitting like bumps on a log—we grow as we wait. If we never had to wait, we would never fully be able to appreciate the gift when it arrives. Waiting isn't God being cruel—it's His kindness. In verse 26, God also explains how when we get tired of waiting, the Holy Spirit steps in to help us. On our own, we will never get this whole waiting-well thing right, but I'm so thankful we don't have to. God provides a helper who comes alongside when we need Him most—whenever the wait seems a little too hard and a little too long.

Making videos of myself has always been a great way for me to process these times of waiting. Talking to my phone and recording myself felt weird at first, but the videos I have made have been such a powerful way for me to remember all that God has done. I love journaling, but the videos have allowed me to see how I was really feeling in any given moment. It's written all over my face. There is no hiding what is really going on. Some videos have been very hard to watch, but most are very encouraging. And I need all the encouragement I can get. I can get discouraged so easily.

Early one morning, I woke up with all kinds of thoughts racing through my mind about waiting. I was right in the middle of dealing with my latest disappointment. I had thought I was about to walk into a relationship with an amazing man, but then, suddenly, it hadn't happened. Instead of my season of waiting being over as I'd dreamed, I found myself right back to staring at a whole lot more waiting. I grabbed my phone and pushed record. Something told me I would want, and most likely *need*, to watch this again later.

As I watch the video now, I see I was still hurting, the pain hadn't just disappeared even though I knew about God's goodness. I also, however, had this faith and confidence shining from my eyes. I still knew God was good. And He would use all the hurt and pain for my good. Somehow.

One of the major things I notice is a lot of my fear had left. I had previously been holding on to the dream of a husband so tightly, because I was afraid it might never happen or wouldn't work out the way I had dreamed. In fact, nothing was happening like I had imagined it. But I was surviving. I know now, even if I never get the thing I want, I will still be okay. That gives me so much courage and strength.

Waiting is sometimes tense and unpleasant, but I am learning my own expectations are being squeezed out of me as I wait—making way for God's truth. The knowledge of that helps me be more open to God's plans over mine. When my hands are open, my loving Father can give me more of Himself. And God is truly all I will ever really need.

Another thing I notice while watching my video is I seemed

to be gaining a greater understanding of surrender. Not getting what I wanted forced me to evaluate where I placed my trust. I'm so thankful for the seasons of hard, because they have taught me God is always trustworthy. There is always that temptation to think I know better, but I hope I can get even better at trusting before I see the promise fulfilled. This type of trust doesn't come without a sense of desperation, and that kind of desperation just wouldn't happen if I always got everything I wanted.

The morning I made this video, I was seeing things through a different filter. What once had felt so dead and hopeless was coming into the light. I could see my waiting time as God did. There wasn't a void of the hard things, but there was also good there and so much hope. The Romans 8 verse was no longer just some verse I had read. Suddenly, it had become so much more. Now I was actually walking it out. I was seeing myself grow as I waited.

I'm so thankful to have those words from Scripture and to have this reminder whenever I need it.

Let's be clear, though, this video and its revelation has not solved everything. I've still had epic meltdowns and pity parties for myself. We must remember that everything is a journey, and there are many things to process. Our lives are filled with many ups and downs, which we must deal with every day. The main thing I hope to accomplish on this journey, however, is to always be growing and to always be getting better and better at turning to Jesus when life gets hard. It's important to cling to His truths and not my earthly desires. Our flesh is so weak, especially when it comes to matters of the heart. We must remind ourselves over and over again that we are enlarged in the waiting. We *grow* during those times of waiting. Get serious about this idea. Say it out loud. Speak it over your situation—repeatedly if you have to until your mood and attitude shifts. We choose what we focus on. Therefore, it's up to us to make sure what we focus on is something *worth* focusing on.

In my video, I also mentioned how God loves us way too much to just give us everything we want. Earthly fathers long to give their children good things but also know giving children everything they ask for can easily turn them into spoiled and selfish people. Also, if a child asks for something dangerous or something that will cause them harm, the earthly father must be judicious with that as well.

> Which of you, if your son asks for bread, will give him a stone? Or if he asks for a fish, will give him a snake? If you, then, though you are evil, know how to give good gifts to your children, how much more will your Father in heaven give good gifts to those who ask him! (Matthew 7:10–11)

This Scripture doesn't say we will get everything we want right when we want it, but it does say our heavenly Father has good gifts for us—another promise we can cling to. Just like the earthly father withholds things that aren't best for his child, we can also count on God to do the same for us. He truly knows what is best for us.

God loves giving us those good gifts, but He focuses more on the process of the waiting and less on the end result. The middle portion of our waiting period is where He refines, shapes, and presses us, so we look more and more like Him in the end. Often this can only happen during moments of waiting. In every case, He uses the waiting for our good. Sometimes the things we want are things God wants for us too, but the timing is not right, and we must wait. I know that is not the fun answer, but it's true.

Once we understand this concept, we can also understand God will not allow us to jump ahead or skip the process. This is part of His deep love for us. We often try to skip ahead when we do it on our own, but we always end up back where we started. God understands how important the process is and that we must traverse through that process in order to obtain true growth and healing.

God knew the periods of waiting wouldn't be easy for us, and so He gave us countless examples in the Bible. There is story after story of people who had to wait for *really* long periods of time to experience the promises God had for them. I find great comfort reading their stories, as it puts purpose to my own setbacks and periods of waiting. The life of Joseph shows this so clearly. God showed him at an early age that he would have great power, but then the wait began. We read stories like this of one event happening after the next and we already know the ending, but can you imagine what the wait must have been like for Joseph? He received a promise from God and then at most points, his life seemed to be going in the opposite direction. Sold into slavery, falsely accused, and even being thrown into prison are not things we often put on the list of what a rise to power looks like. These situations ended up being exactly what God would use to prepare him for all that was to come. Even through all the twists and turns, God had a plan.

He also has a plan for you. I know the waiting often feels discouraging and more like a setback, but it will all be for your good. Just like He did with Joseph, God is using this season to prepare you for all that is to come.

Along with making videos of myself, I also love to journal. More specifically I love to write letters. Most of the time I pen letters to the Lord. They are such a good outlet to help me process through my feelings. Other times I have done the opposite and written what I imagined the Lord would say to me if He were writing me a letter. These letters have been so special to me and have proved to be a great way for me to remember God's goodness.

As I was sitting on a beach one morning journaling, I asked God what He thought of me. I could hear God's response as I wrote. "My most precious daughter, oh, how I love you! I love watching you grow and take flight. I know the journey wasn't always easy, but I hope you've been able to see that I never left you, and I've always wanted what was best for you. I've seen the long, hard nights, and trust me, they were hard for me to watch, but I love you way too much to rush anything. I always have and I always will have a plan for all of it."

"For I know the plans I have for you," declares the Lord, "plans to prosper you and not to harm you, plans to give you hope and a future. Then you will call on me and come and pray to me, and I will listen to you." (Jeremiah 29:11)

These words from my heavenly Father mean so much to me. He knows my pain and hurt intimately, because He has been there with me through it all, listening to each and every prayer. But He loves me too much to rush anything. And He feels the exact same way about you. He sees and knows the full picture when we only see small parts of it. Sometimes there is nothing else we can do but just trust Him.

In addition, waiting makes the result that much sweeter. A great example of this came to me one day on the way to work.

I don't know a ton about music, and I know zero details of what goes into writing a song. What I do know is I love the bridge part of a song. Once it happens you can't help but dance or turn up the music in your car, so you can sing at the top of your lungs. When the bridge moment happens, my car concert really gets good.

On one particular morning, I was listening to my radio—I don't remember what song—and I remember thinking, *Maybe I should just fast-forward to the part when it really gets good.* I was in the mood to sing my heart out, so I went straight to the bridge. When I did that, I had an epiphany of sorts. The bridge wasn't nearly as powerful when I skipped to it.

The beginning of a song contains the building blocks that lead the listener to the big bridge moment. It's this building up that makes that moment so powerful. By skipping ahead, I had deprived myself of the bridge's full impact. The beginning of the song serves a purpose. Without it there would be no big moment. I couldn't wait to get to work and write this revelation down. The waiting serves a purpose, and without it I wouldn't be able to fully enjoy the thing I had waited on. A deep appreciation is built during the times of waiting. I believe marriage is in my future, and, boy, is it ever going to be that much sweeter thanks to the wait.

Knowing this reality doesn't mean I don't wish there were another way. I wish I could learn these lessons without having to wait and without going through the hard times, but that's very unlikely. In addition, if I weren't going through the pain of continuing to wait, I might not have obtained these moments of growth and clarity in my life.

I hope things are starting to come into focus a little more for you. I hope you are starting to see that the wait is not an awful thing happening to you but rather an incredible blessing. There are so many factors at play, and we will never know half of them. The ways of the Lord are different from our ways (Isaiah 55:9). But here is what I do know: God has wonderful things in store for us as we wait. He doesn't just make us wait for waiting's sake. He has a very clear and specific purpose in mind. We don't always get to know what those things are in the moment, but when we look back after waiting, we realize we are stronger and more equipped to deal with whatever is coming next. Now that is a good Father.

This wait that we all hate so much is absolutely in your favor.

Let's Get *Real*

- How are you experiencing the Holy Spirit helping you through your season of waiting? And if you need more of His help, take a moment to ask Him.
- In what ways have you seen yourself enlarged in the waiting?
- Ask God how He feels about you and how He sees this season of waiting. Give Him time to speak and then write down what He says. You will want to remember it.
- God longs to be in the waiting with you. Take a moment to invite Him into your current situation. Surrender your desires and expectations to Him.

Dad, I just read that this wait that I hate so much might actually be in my favor, but I don't honestly believe that is true. Can you show me that you will use all of it for my good? Your Word also promises that you come alongside me and help as needed, and I need you so desperately. My heart is heavy and burdened and I could really use some encouragement. Can you tell me what you think about this season of waiting? All I see is the hard, but I want to see your goodness in there too. I am here willing to listen, will you please speak to me?

And then sit and really listen. Grab a pen and paper and write down whatever you believe the Holy Spirit is saying to you. Try to not think so hard about each word; just let the pen do more of the talking. I'm praying that you find encouragement and peace right in this very moment.

Chapter 4

Handing Over the Veil

*Y*ou might be thinking, "Okay, so if all this is true, is it okay to desire that thing I'm waiting on? Or does truly trusting God mean I need to stop hoping for it completely? And is it possible to hold on to the desire but also to be content at the same time?"

I have wrestled with these same questions. At times, I have felt shame for my desire to be married. Perhaps it was wrong to hope for marriage, or maybe I hoped for it too much. When the thing we hope for doesn't come to fruition in our time frame, we start to think maybe we shouldn't have hoped for it in the first place.

I have been healthy and unhealthy in my desires. I have tried to ignore them, and I have also tried to pretend they didn't exist, which only seemed to leave me more miserable. My desires persisted whether I chose to accept them or tried to ignore them. During some of my unhealthiest times, I have sat in bitterness and anger.

Anger can be a good thing because it pushes us toward change, but it can also really hurt us if we decide to sit in that anger and not deal with it. I don't know about you, but I have thrown some of the most epic pity parties. Most of the time, those moments involved me telling anyone and everyone who would listen how bad my life was. I thought it would make me feel better if everyone knew just how hard it had been for me to wait. I believed getting sympathy from people would somehow make me feel better. It might have felt like it helped for a short time, but I would eventually feel bad again. When I look back on those times, I can also see staying in that place of bitterness didn't help me at all.

In those moments I couldn't really see around the desire. My dreams became my focus and took up so much of my time and attention. At first I didn't even realize I was doing this. But over time, so many of my thoughts ended with the phrase *when I get married.* It was almost as if my life paused, and my emotions and thoughts made me believe getting married was the only way it would begin again. My desire became so strong it began to feel more like a *need* and not just something I *really wanted.* I *needed* to be married to really be happy. I *needed* to get married, so my life could really start. I *needed* to get married, because then I would know God was good. Somehow, I had missed that God is good *all the time.* He is who He says He is and not because He gives me what I want.

If these emotions sound similar to thoughts you've been experiencing, then there might be something unhealthy going on, and you might need to address the situation.

But how do we even do that?

First, we have to be willing to tell the truth. Ignoring a problem is never going to make it go away. We have to be willing to admit something is going on. I would even suggest going a step further and sharing it with someone you can trust. Not everyone is safe to share intimate details with, and that is okay. But it is so helpful if you can find at least one person you can be completely honest with. Speaking those things out loud and bringing them into the light is often healing. Situations tend to build up in our minds, but when we share them with someone else, they no longer have as much power over us.

Second, take them to Jesus. We must hand over these desires to the only person who knows what to do with them. The one who loves us more than anyone else. The one who knows what is best for us and will always have our best interests in mind. God alone knows what to do with our desires, and He knows exactly the right time to give them back to us or if we should get them back at all. Remember, He only wants to give us the best gifts.

Third, find out what the Word says about how you're feeling. You may not feel like reading God's Word or praying—especially if you feel abandoned by God—but we must read it if we want to live our fullest and best lives. I'm not suggesting you spend time in the Word because it's on your Christian checklist, but I'm saying you must spend time in the Word because it has the power to change your situation. It's the truth you need in your most painful moments. When our hearts are hemorrhaging, sometimes the last thing we want to do is read the Bible. Again, we can't forget there is an enemy who wants only to *steal, kill, and destroy* (John 10:10). Of course, the Enemy tries to keep us from reading the Word. He knows how powerful the Word of God is and also how helpful it is. Even if all you can do is read one verse over and over, start there. Pick out a promise, and say it out loud. Doing that one small thing can be enough to change your mindset, remind you of God's goodness, and bring healing into your situation. God's Word is a powerful weapon. We must fight through the lies and use the tools we have been given.

Here's the deal, I won't pretend to have all the answers or that I know exactly how to navigate holding on to my desires. I do, however, believe as I have wrestled with these questions, that God has graciously shown me a few things, and I want to share them with you.

A major thing I have learned is this: if it doesn't go against the

Word of God, your desire isn't bad. For example, the Word doesn't say that money itself is bad or having money is bad. The Bible does say, however, that the *love of money* is a root of all kinds of evil (1 Timothy 6:10). It isn't our desire that's necessarily bad—it's when we place that desire above and before God in our lives. Our joy and peace can't be dependent on all our dreams or desires coming true. Our joy and peace come from God alone. The Lord wants us to entrust our desires to Him, to trust Him with them, and to not try to twist or manipulate things simply to achieve what we want. When we can do that, our desires take their proper place in our lives. We don't have to deny or ignore our desires, but they can't take the number-one spot in our lives either.

My church used to do early morning prayer on Wednesday mornings, but I am not a morning person. (Those that have been fortunate enough to see me early in the morning know this to be true.) When my alarm went off each Wednesday, the struggle was very real for me. Each time I made the effort, however, the Lord always showed up too and honored my sacrifice (because that's what He does). In addition, there was something so sacred about those Wednesday mornings. Perhaps it was because my mind wasn't fully awake yet, and therefore, I struggled less with my own desires and was able to focus on Jesus more. I put Him first in my day, and He met me at the center of my need each time.

One Wednesday morning during my personal prayer time, I thought about sacrifice and how hard it often is. I had watched a video on surrender the night before, so this concept was fresh in my mind. The person in the video talked about how terrifying it often is to give up control—to completely and fully open our hands and let go of those desires when we have been holding on so tightly to that thing we really want. To say, "Okay, God, I'm giving it to you." I loved hearing that letting go of things was hard for someone else too. That gave me so much freedom to acknowledge that I am also not good at giving up control.

Many times, my counselor has made this profound statement:

"There are no *shoulds*." This is her way of encouraging me to let go of the ideas of how I think I'm supposed to be doing things. When it comes to surrender, I feel so many *shoulds*.

I feel like I *should* want to gladly give up control. I feel like I *should* trust Jesus more. I feel like letting go of my desires *should* be easier. I feel like I *should* not feel any fear around letting go. I feel like I *should* handle the situation more like my friend—she always seems to get it right. I do this so often. I have so many ideas of how I *should* do things, and when I miss that mark, I often get frustrated or feel shame. I have this deep desire to get it right. Say the right things. Do the right things. Act in a manor worthy of being called a Christian.

There is so much pressure. All the time.

If you need the reminder like I do, let me help you out. There are no *shoulds*. If giving up control is hard for you too, know you are not alone.

Here is another thing: Jesus knows giving up control is hard for us. He isn't offended or mad because we feel it's hard to lay our desires down. He doesn't stand off in the distance judging. Instead, He steps into the darkness with us and offers love and understanding. He's never expected us to be perfect; that is something only we expect of ourselves.

> For we do not have a high priest who is unable to sympathize with our weaknesses, but we have one who has been tempted in every way, just as we are—yet was without sin. (Hebrews 4:15)

On this particular Wednesday morning, as I was praying, I tried to let these truths wash over me. I got this picture in my head of being in a room with Jesus. I knew I was holding on very tightly to something, but Jesus stood before me so peacefully. I was standing there feeling worried and stressed, but He was still so peaceful.

He didn't rush to me or plead with me. He didn't try to grab the thing I'd been holding on to out of my hand or wrestle it out of my grasp. He simply stood there and waited for me to make my choice—there was so much love in His eyes as He looked at me.

I realized I had a decision to make. I could hand over this thing I had been holding on to, which I knew represented my desire to be married, or I could continue to hold on to it. As I thought about this scenario playing itself out, I realized it was a wedding veil I was holding. This made so much sense, because I had been dreaming about wearing my mom's veil at my wedding. For so many reasons, this veil felt sacred and special. In this moment, I felt like I had to give it up. Letting go of my dream terrified me, but I quickly realized Jesus wasn't asking me to give up my desire to be married. He was, however, asking me to give up control of that dream. To move away from the worry and from the fear of not getting married—to not let it consume me—and instead, to turn toward Him. To trust God could take care of it for me.

I handed over the veil to Jesus in my mind, and what I saw next meant so much to me. He didn't grab the veil and just throw it down. He took that veil lovingly, with so much tenderness and so much care. Then He folded it and put the veil gently on a shelf behind Him. His actions showed me He understood how much the veil meant to me and how hard it had been to hand it over.

I imagined Him saying, "I know that was hard, and I know how much this means to you. I am not taking this away from you, but I'm so thankful you decided to give it to me. I know what to do with it. I know how to fold it just right, and I can keep it just where it needs to be. I know exactly what needs to be done before I give it back to you. You can trust me. I know the exact right moment to give it back to you."

In that moment, I sensed He valued my desire by taking the utmost care of it. I knew He also wouldn't withhold it forever. He simply put it away for safekeeping.

Did you catch what He *didn't* say? He didn't make me feel bad for wanting the thing in the first place. He didn't shame me. He also didn't try to make me feel bad because it had taken me so long to give this special item to Him. I only heard and saw love and understanding in His actions.

We do not need to ignore our desires or throw them away like trash. We need only to hand them over to the one who really knows how to take care of them. The one who knows the right moment to return them to us.

The God who created the universe and yet still knows every hair on your head can handle every one of your dreams and desires.

Here is another thing I learned: this is not a once-and-done situation. We all love a quick fix. We are eager to cross things off the list and not have to think about them again. But surrender needs to happen over and over again daily, sometimes even moment by moment. If you start to feel sad or angry about this surrender, remember, it's not that you did something wrong—only that your fleshly desires are strong. Throw off that shame as quickly as you can, and hand your desires back to Jesus again. Continue to give it to God as many times as you must. And know that it will get easier and will be worth it over time.

Here is another cool part. This daily surrender isn't a road to less but, in fact, it leads to more.

I used to believe if I completely gave up control, it would mean I no longer would be able to have any fun. All that would be left is to follow a list of rules. I also genuinely believed if I gave something over to God, He would give me something I didn't like in return. If I didn't personally choose my husband, God would give me someone I wasn't even attracted to. I absolutely didn't understand who God was.

As I have gotten to know God's character better, I have learned giving up control won't give me less in return. Instead, giving up control clears everything out of the way, so I can enjoy the freedom and fullness that God always intended me to experience—not following a set of rules but living in abundance under His protective guidelines. He wants that for you so badly, but He knows you can't walk in that kind of abundance while trying to be in control. He wants you to live a life free of worry, but that can only happen when you trust Him and His plan for you.

It's so very freeing to know I don't have to be in control all the time. I don't have to worry if He has marriage waiting for me. I don't have to worry about finding the perfect husband. I don't have to worry about the timing or if I'll be too old to carry a child. I also don't have to worry about life moving in the opposite direction of where I think it should go. When I give up control, I start to feel so much freedom. Giving up control means I am trusting God and I don't have to worry anymore. And I learn when the Word says we will be kept in "perfect peace" when we put our trust in God (Isaiah 26:3), it's really true. Providing the peace isn't our job. Our part is simply giving up control. God's job is to do everything else. He does all the heavy lifting, which includes working all the details out for us. We don't have to figure anything out. We simply trust God has our best interests in mind. The God who created the entire universe will literally move heaven and earth to make sure His perfect will comes to pass. This is how we can sleep easy even as we wait.

I find anxiety can really creep in when I spend my time asking the "how" questions or when I try to make a plan for how something will happen. For example, I believe I will get married one day. I believe that is a God given desire and it is beautiful. What is not so beautiful is when I make all kinds of assumptions or plans about how it will happen. When I decide the best path to marriage, I get myself in all kinds of trouble. I become frustrated when things don't go according to my plans and worry seems to take over when things take longer than I think they should.

God gives us the dreams and shows us where we are going, which is so gracious of Him. But then we often try to run ahead and figure out exactly how we are going to get there. We fail to remember God will also illuminate each step along the way. No need to figure out the timeline or how your story will look. God knows how you will get to the end, and He will lead you one step at a time. When we try to control how we will get there, we are not walking in that "perfect peace."

Giving up control also allows God to work in ways we never could. Our human minds and resources are limited, so there is only so much we can do. We can try as hard as we can, do everything right, and still never come close to what God can do. When we surrender control, He is free to do the work only He can. He sees the entire picture when we only see a very small part. Only in our heavenly Father's hands can the Enemy's attempt to harm us be turned around for good. Because He's so gracious, He even turns around the bad things we brought upon ourselves. His promise to each of us is that He will use *all* of it for our good.

But His hands are tied if you do not give over control. That is a decision only you can make. It will not always be easy, but it will be worth it every time.

One of the main questions I've spent tons of time mulling over in my mind is: can I desire marriage but also be content in my singleness at the same time? I have often wondered if these two things can coexist. Again, I don't have all the answers, but I do think it's possible. In fact, in the Bible we see this was the case for Adam. He was fully satisfied and had an unhindered, intimate relationship with God in the garden. Yet even God acknowledged there was something missing. There was no helper suitable for Adam. God would later take care of the need, but for a time, Adam was fully satisfied and yet still had a longing. This will always be our reality as well. There is always going to be struggle and longing in one form or another in our lives. We work so hard to avoid struggle or work our way to a place where it no longer exists. Here on earth, however, the absence of struggle will never be possible. Our hearts were created to desire a perfection that won't happen until eternity. Therefore, we will always be living somewhere in the middle of the tension of right now and not yet. We will never be truly satisfied, because we were made for more than we are experiencing right now. We were made for things to come.

This might seem like an act of cruelty to you, but there is another lens to view the situation through. God loves you so much that He created an eternity for you. He knows our human bodies are frail and weak. Therefore, our time here on earth is not forever. Even as we speak, He is preparing a place for us in heaven. It would really be cruel if we had to stay in this frail state forever. But your heavenly Father loves you too much to leave you here forever.

He also loves you too much to leave you alone in the hard situations of today. He has given us His Word and the Holy Spirit to help us walk through this life. Both show us how to best live and deal with the longings.

When we bring our desires to the Father, we find peace—not because the struggle is somehow gone, but because we see God is bigger than the struggle. When we start to see inside the center of His will, He can help us manage the struggle. Each day we must decide if we can dare to believe that even in this God has a plan. That's when the peace that passes all understanding floods our circumstances, when we can trust God has a plan even while we are still waiting.

In case you hadn't realized it yet, I love to ask the Lord these kinds of hard questions. The Bible is such a great resource to find the answers to our questions, but the Holy Spirit also longs to talk directly to us. I like to ask the questions and wait for the answers. Sometimes they come right away, or sometimes it's much later. I won't even begin to try to figure out why that is the case. I know, however, God longs for relationship with us, and therefore, I always seem to get an answer. One day, as I was stretching before a workout, I asked Him, "How do I hold my desires for the things I want and also be content with where I am today?"

In this instance, the answer came so quickly; I grabbed my phone and started typing:

You trust Me. You wake up every day acknowledging that there is a desire there, and you place it in My hands. When you really place it in My hands, you don't pretend it isn't there, you don't beg Me to not feel anything, and you don't try to twist and manipulate the situation to get that thing you want. And that unmet desire, it's a gift that draws you close to Me. And then as you put down the desire, you get to walk forward into your day, and I'll show you how to live it well. It's not giving up on the dream, but it's also not holding on to it so tightly that you can see nothing else. You give it to me, and I work out all the details, and that opens your eyes to seeing the gift that is today.

I loved the response, because it was filled with so much love and understanding. This is how the Father always responds to us, never condemning and always pointing us back to truth. His response was also such a good reminder of the daily surrender that needs to take place.

It's not easy, but there are wonderful gifts waiting for us when we give up control. They might not look exactly like we thought they would, but most of the time they are even better. We will never be fully satisfied on earth, but being aware of that need and being willing to hand it over to Jesus allows us to experience moments of deep gratification today. And that is true contentment.

Let's Get *Real*

- There are no *shoulds.* What are some *shoulds* you've allowed into your life? Write them down so you can see them and then more easily let them go.
- Is there anything you need to hand over to Jesus? If something comes to mind that seems terrifying to give up control of, then that might be the very thing you need to let go of.
- We were made of things to come. How are you living in the *already* and *not yet?* Jot down some promises God has given you for today, and some things God has promised for the future.

Father, there are so many things I believe I should do, but each time I miss the mark, I feel so much shame. The weight of trying to get it right all the time is exhausting. Can you help lift the weight? Can you remind me that you never asked perfection of me? I know I have been holding on so tightly to my desire to be married. It's often so hard and confusing that my biggest desire has gone unmet. In this moment I want to stand on your truth and not the hard. Even before I fully believe it, I choose to say that your will is better than mine and I can trust you. I can give up control. I place my desires in your capable hands, and I trust that you know exactly what to do with them. I believe even in this, you have a plan.

Chapter 5

Purpose to the Pain

*E*ver wondered if we can just skip over the hard stuff? Must we endure the hurt and pain? Or is there another way around? If we ignore our feelings for long enough, will they just go away?

I really wish I could give you another answer, one that you would be more excited to hear. The truth is we can't skip the hard places and truly thrive like God created us to. We can try with all our might, but true healing won't take place unless we face the difficult times too. Emotions never dealt with will only sit there and fester. We must be willing to feel them and work our way through them. Remember, God is a God of the process. He loves us too much to let us skip ahead. Also, our feelings do not go away simply because we ignore them. They will still surface at some point. This could happen in prayer, in a counselor's office, with a trusted friend, or it could happen in an epic explosion. Often when feelings aren't addressed, they cause us to lash out. Unfortunately, all too often, it happens with the people we love the most.

On the other side of things, not accepting and addressing our emotions can lead to depression. If we stuff our feelings inside long enough, we end up in a state of numbness, no longer able to feel much of anything.

Again, I really wish there were a more fun answer for you, but I hope God will show you there is purpose to the pain. I pray you will know walking through the hard is worth it, and there will be so much good that comes from enduring.

I used to think feeling my feelings was bad. I have always been an emotional person, and I think I learned at a young age that it was best if I kept my emotions in check. This thought process eventually led me to believe I shouldn't feel any of the negative emotions. I believed no matter what I was feeling, I should keep it together on the outside. I saw anger and sadness as negative emotions and felt shame for feeling them. I still have a hard time with anger actually. Feeling angry, however, can be such a good thing, because it can push us to make much-needed changes in our lives. Once we become angry enough, we often do something about it.

But anger had such a negative connotation in my mind. I felt shame every time I got angry, which only compounded my already overly emotional mind. I didn't realize there was a healthy way to deal with my emotions; I just believed I shouldn't feel them.

I also thought if I was sad it must mean God wasn't good. I felt like I was supposed to slap "God is good" on top of whatever hard thing I was going through. No need to feel sad, because *God is good.* That situation really shouldn't be that difficult, because *God is good.* Just wipe the tears, smile, nod, and say, "God is good."

As you have already read, I do believe *God is good* and that will never change. Whether I am sad, joyful, angry, or glad . . . His goodness doesn't change! But He also knows we are very much human with very real emotions. Therefore, He doesn't expect us to pretend our feelings don't exist.

I see now how my previous logic was a little off. It has taken time and many counseling sessions for me to change some of those old thought patterns. I have begun to realize my emotions do have a place and they are not bad. I've also learned that I am not weak or less than when I do have emotions. Sure, there is a healthy and unhealthy way to deal with them, but having emotions and allowing myself to feel them isn't wrong. And it most certainly does not make me weak.

Jesus even set this example for us in the garden of Gethsemane. The Bible says He was in such agony that His sweat fell to the ground like drops of blood (Luke 22:44). He was about to go through the most horrific experience of His life. He trusted His Father; therefore, He knew this hard moment served a greater purpose. He knew the sacrifice was necessary. He always knew it was His destiny. And yet, He still had feelings about what was about to happen. Even though He was fully God, we see in this moment that He was also fully human. If Jesus, who never sinned, never disappointed His Father, and always did His Father's will, felt His emotions that night in the garden, I'm pretty sure it is okay for us to feel our emotions too. I would never try to compare what we are going through to what Jesus felt that night, but my point is that it wasn't a sin for Him to have feelings about what was about to happen.

What would have been a sin is if Jesus were to have followed His emotions, decided it was too much to handle, and turned away from the cross. Can you imagine how strange it would have been to hear Jesus say He just didn't *feel* like doing it, so He was no longer going to? He didn't let His emotions get the best of Him, and He didn't change His mind because of them. But He did feel them. He went to His Father and expressed an emotion so deep we may never understand it.

Let me say this to you with deep love: you are not bad or wrong because you have feelings. You are human. Your feelings and emotions are a large part of what makes you . . . you. And God loves you so much. Those emotions you often hate can be such gifts. If we never knew deep sorrow, we would never be able to experience the richness of joy. Your emotions serve a purpose, and you aren't wrong for feeling them.

There are, however, healthy and unhealthy ways to express these emotions. Often our emotions can be great indicators of what is going on, but they aren't what we should base our actions or decisions on. Let me explain. If I feel angry because of something someone has done to me, I have a choice about how to respond. I can lash out and yell at the person—which often turns into a hurtful name-calling event—or I can acknowledge the anger and realize I am feeling it because I am experiencing hurt. Whatever that person did has hurt me, and I need to address that hurt. It's okay to feel the hurt and to have emotions around that, but lashing out at the person who hurt you will not be helpful for anyone.

Once upon a time, a similar scenario happened to me. (My emotions have often gotten the best of me, and I have lashed out at people more times than I want to even think about.) This instance occurred when I wasn't invited to my ex boyfriend's wedding. I know what you are thinking . . . I shouldn't even *want* to go to his wedding anyway. You also might be thinking, *Duh, of course he didn't invite you. Why would he?* But here's the thing: we have been best friends since the fifth grade. My mom and his mom were best friends, and our families are deeply connected because of that. Our moms threw us a joint sweet-sixteen party. We also had a joint graduation party when we graduated high school. Therefore, I couldn't imagine missing this milestone in his life. Everyone told me not to expect the invitation, but again, I'm a dreamer. I just knew he would still invite me. Fantasy land is so nice!

But he didn't invite me. Which was totally his and his soon-to-be-wife's choice and was possibly for the best (or something). But you better believe I still had all kinds of feelings about it. My first thought was to call him and let him have a piece of my mind.

This probably would not have been helpful. (I'm grateful for the moments I stop and think a little more before I just react based on my emotions.) I also wanted to call him and let him know he made a mistake. Also, not helpful. Or maybe, I thought, I should just call him and get him to change his mind. Again, not a good plan. I kept hearing my counselor's voice in my head, which was equally helpful and annoying. She had talked me off many ledges in the past and helped show me healthy ways to deal with my feelings. I knew the things I wanted to do in this situation would not fall on the "healthy ways to deal with my feelings" list.

The next week I was still feeling frustrated, sad, and disappointed. I decided to process these feelings with my counselor. She listened and spoke truth to me, like she always does. She reminded me this wedding wasn't about me at all. Okay ouch . . . not what I wanted to hear. But she was right. I needed to be reminded of that. She didn't discredit my feelings that day, but she did go a step further and ask me if I knew any healthy ways I could process what I was feeling. Through clenched teeth, I told her I thought it would be a good idea to give myself time to journal and get all my feelings out. She agreed, and I thought, *Great, another thing to feel.* At this point I knew letting myself fully feel my emotions had been very helpful for me, but it was also not something I was excited about.

After I was done being mad, which took several more days, I set aside some time to journal and process. I went out onto my porch, turned on worship music, and started writing. I just let it all out. What I wrote wasn't pretty or polished, but I wrote down everything I was really feeling. I wrote how I was sad and hurt and just wished everything could be different.

In the middle of letting all my feelings out, something crazy happened . . . I started to feel better. Before I knew it, my writing turned into this beautiful reminder that God had never let me down before, and I could trust Him in this situation too.

On my ex's wedding day, I happened to be house hunting in

Nashville. When I thought about this fact later that day, I realized I was exactly where I needed to be, and everything had worked out after all.

Sitting in my feelings for a set amount of time and journaling about them has been so helpful. In this case, journaling was all I needed to do. There are instances, however, when more needs to be done. Some wounds and hurts are so deep they will take a lot more time to heal. You might have to revisit them over and over in order to bring true healing. Each situation is so unique, and how you process might be totally different than how I deal with my emotions. The important thing is that you process. And that you try to find a healthy way to do so. This is something that doesn't just happen. We don't automatically know how to deal with our emotions in healthy ways. But it is something we can learn.

All this might sound good to you, but you also might be wondering why we have to experience pain at all. Can something that feels so bad really serve a purpose? Why would a good God allow us to feel such deep hurt?

Pain serves a purpose, and God uses all of it for our good.

It's often easier for us to understand this concept when we think of physical pain serving a purpose. Pain is part of our body's warning system. It lets us know something isn't right. It says there is a problem that needs to be fixed. One of my best friends is a nurse in a pediatric clinic. She explained to me they encourage the parents of their patients not to give their children Tylenol around the clock. When pain meds are given that often, they could mask a fever. And a fever signals that something is wrong. There is purpose to the pain.

Imagine you have a sprained ankle. I'm guessing your doctor would tell you to take some amount of pain medicine, but if you take too much, you run the risk of feeling no pain at all. If that happens, you might push yourself too hard, which then might cause you to hurt yourself again or possibly prolong the healing of the original injury. The pain lets us know we need to rest, to stay off that ankle, to give it time to heal. There is purpose to the pain.

Pain is what caused doctors to first find my mom's cancer. She wasn't having any major symptoms until one night she started having excruciating pain in her abdomen. That pain caused my parents to rush to the hospital where doctors eventually discovered the cancer. Cancer did ultimately take her life, but not until twelve years after this first diagnosis. The pain helped everyone catch the cancer before it was too late. The pain gave us twelve more years with my mom. That pain allowed her to be at high school and college graduations, almost every one of my college softball games, and at the birth of both my nieces. There is purpose to the pain.

This same truth also applies to emotional pain. If there is hurt or pain of any kind, it is a warning signal there is something that needs to be addressed. That hurt you feel isn't accidental—it's there to let you know something isn't right. Sometimes our feelings are valid, and sometimes they have no validity at all. Either way, I suggest you still deal with them. Sometimes that wound is fresh, and sometimes it's been there so long, the pain feels more like a friend. The time or severity of the wound isn't what matters. The time for healing and dealing with your wounds could be right in this moment. We often downplay what is going on and talk ourselves out of dealing with the pain. But it's never too late, and there is no pain that is too small to address. If it is hurting us, God cares about all of it.

As I was writing this chapter, I was going through my friend Ann Goering's new Bible study, called *Betrothed*. This study explains how we can know if we have a wound that needs healing. "You can tell the wound is gaping by what's coming out of it. If it's festering fear, unforgiveness, bitterness, retaliation, unkindness, impatience, entitlement or retribution,"[3] then it's highly likely some healing needs to take place.

---

[3] Ann Goering, *Betrothed* (Branson, Missouri: Covered Porch Publishing, 2019).

Here's the best news. God can heal even the deepest hurts and wounds. Not one thing we go through or are feeling falls outside His capable hands. We aren't, however, always willing to let Him do the work. We hide, pull away, numb the pain, or try to pretend we are holding it all together. Let me just remove that pressure. You don't have to keep it together. You don't have to hide. The Enemy wants you to feel shame and to believe that healing isn't possible. But that's a lie. God is always willing to help heal your pain. He's so able to heal the pain. And He wants you to experience true and total healing.

This is His promise to you, yes you, even today, even now:

> The righteous cry out, and the Lord hears them; he delivers them from all their troubles. The Lord is close to the brokenhearted and saves those who are crushed in spirit. The righteous person may have many troubles, but the Lord delivers him from them all; he protects all his bones, not one of them will be broken. (Psalm 34:17–20)

This verse isn't just for people who have no problems and have it all together. It isn't just for pastors. It isn't just for people on stage, leading people. This is a promise for all of us. God will be near when we are brokenhearted, and He will save those who feel crushed in spirit. His Word says He will deliver us from *all* our troubles. That includes whatever you are going through and whatever hurt you are feeling *right now*. You can face the pain, and you can trust Jesus will be right there walking you through it.

Sometimes addressing the pain makes it feel worse. When the pain is at its worst point, most of us begin to feel like it's too hard or maybe not worth it to try and move on. We often give up right before we reach the point of full freedom and total healing.

My head had been hurting for weeks. When I went to bed at

night, I had a headache. When I woke up in the morning, I had a headache. Going to the doctor is such a pain to me, and I always assume there is nothing they can do anyway, so I just kept thinking the pain would eventually go away. After three weeks of this pain, I started to think maybe something more serious was going on. Eventually, I got to the point where I could no longer deal with the headache. I finally decided to see the doctor. (Don't be like me. If your body is signaling you that something is wrong, go get it checked out.) Thankfully, after some tests and a thorough exam, the doctor told me the pain was associated with a problem with my shoulder. Although I had been having weird shoulder issues off and on, it hadn't been hurting this time, so I didn't even think about it being related. My doctor suggested getting a massage and seeing a chiropractor. If those things didn't help, I would see him again.

I followed the doctor's orders and had a massage and also went to the chiropractor a few times, but I didn't feel any better. In fact, I actually felt worse. My shoulder now felt agitated in addition to my head hurting even more than it did before. At that point I could have decided it was hopeless and stopped the chiropractor appointments. I could have decided the additional pain wasn't worth it and that I would just live with the current level of headaches and pain.

This might sound ridiculous to you, but we jump to those kinds of conclusions all the time when it comes to emotional pain. I went to counseling once, and I felt worse, so it must not be working. I tried to talk to my family member about my true feelings, and the discussion went horribly—I'm never doing that again. I feel sad and angry all the time, but I already know nothing will help, so I'll just live with it. No one knows what they really did to me, and it would hurt way too much to forgive them, so I'm just going to hold on to this bitterness. I feel sad and frustrated, and I've waited for so long, God must not be good.

Know that if you have been working your way through some kind of pain, and it almost feels like it has gotten worse, you are not alone. What you are going through is totally normal. Healing doesn't look the same for everyone and doesn't occur in one straight line. You might take a huge leap forward one day, only to feel worse the next. It might be two steps forward and one step back. But you will get to total healing—give it time.

Even though it might not feel like it, God will give you the strength to keep going and to keep enduring whatever it is you're dealing with. Please, don't give up. The Enemy will try to convince you that your previous time of suffering wasn't that bad. And at times, it will feel much easier to run back to your old patterns. Those patterns appear safe and comfortable, but they really aren't. They are slowly but surely leading to death and destruction in areas of your life. Don't let the emotions you are feeling today have the final say. I know they feel very real and true, but they are fleeting. Hold on to the promises in the Word and the hope that is Jesus. I promise you can do this. I promise you won't be alone. God is with you . . . always!

Start by asking God what a good next step would be for you. He longs to provide guidance for us. I can't promise you when or what it will look like, but I believe He will answer you. Perhaps He will lead you to a counselor. Maybe He'll encourage you to tell someone else what is going on so they can encourage you and provide accountability. Perhaps journaling will help. Maybe sitting on the floor crying and simply letting it all come out will be most beneficial. It might mean having a tough conversation with someone you love. It might be finding a church so you can be a part of an authentic body of believers—a church full of other messed-up people trying to allow God to help them look more like Jesus too.

I have no idea what the next step is for you, but please don't give up or walk away right before you get to the good stuff. It's time to take the next step.

In case you are wondering, I stuck it out with the chiroprac-tor and got a couple more massages, and eventually the pain and the headaches did go away. It would have been pretty silly for me to decide to simply live with the pain when I could have done something about it. This applies to the emotional wounds that are still festering as well. Your pain might become more difficult, and it might take a while to feel or see anything changing, but it will eventually get better. I know that to be true firsthand, and it is true for you as well.

In the middle of my depression, I had resolved that I was meant to be the sad girl, and I started identifying with that title. I had been through so much, and I had decided I would always be sad. I didn't see any way around it. Now, knowing I didn't stay in that place brings tears to my eyes. As I brought all that sadness to the Lord, through time He allowed me to see I wasn't the sad girl. God had never called me the sad girl. He called me *beloved, chosen,* and *beautiful.* Now I experience so much joy on a daily basis—not the kind of joy that's based on my circumstances, but the true and deep joy that comes from knowing God is with me and will take care of me. That kind of joy remains, even while I am still hurting and experiencing pain.

The journey to healing is not always simple, and I know the road I'm asking you to venture out on is not an easy one to walk. But friends, it is worth it. Dealing with your pain, letting the Lord uncover the true source of that pain, and acknowledging the wound so you can eventually let it go will always be worth it. There will always be a point to that kind of work, and you will always be thankful you did it.

There will also always be a purpose to the pain. The pain will always make us acutely aware of our need for a savior. The good news is we already have one. He has already done everything necessary for you to experience uninhibited joy and freedom no matter what you face.

Let the pain do its work. Let it be a giant arrow pointing you to Jesus. Because He loves you more than you can fathom, He will redeem every second of the pain. That's who He is, and that's what He does. All that you are facing today will be the foundation you stand on tomorrow. The exact spot of your pain could end up being the very spot something so beautiful grows.

There is purpose to the pain, and God will make sure not an ounce of it is wasted.

Let's Get *Real*

- Do you have any wounds or pain that you have been ignoring? The Holy Spirit may be bringing something to your mind now. If He hasn't, stop and ask if Him if there is any pain that you need to deal with.
- What is a next step you can take to start dealing with that pain? If nothing comes to mind, ask God to show you something you can do.

Father, please show me if there is any pain I am experiencing that I need to deal with. I'm starting to understand that you want me to address it so that I can experience freedom and healing. So, will you show me what that pain point is? What is causing the pain? Give me insight into the root of the pain, and then can you show me the next step to take? Thank you for being my healer and loving me enough to help me uncover the pain. I know it isn't easy to watch your daughter hurting, but I trust your love for me and that there will be something good waiting for me on the other side. I am weak, and I know I will want to run back to old habits so quickly. But can you be strong for me? I am taking the next step into the unknown, and even though I might not always see it, I am going to believe that you will help me walk in total healing and freedom. Thank you for the pain, and thank you for redeeming all the hard.

Chapter 6

What I Thought, Was Not

Ever had something all planned out in your head and then watched it all fall apart? Have you ever been in a relationship you were certain would end in marriage, but it didn't? Ever thought a relationship was about to happen only to realize the feelings weren't reciprocated? I, too, have experienced being so certain I knew how something would work out only to realize *what I thought, was not.*

One of my besties and I have been saying that phrase to one another a lot lately. I'm pretty sure in the beginning we repeated the phrase, simply so I didn't burst into tears. We often made jokes about how we could write a whole sermon series on the topic of not getting what we thought we were getting. Just one sermon wouldn't be enough.

One night, we were talking about *what I thought, was not* in front of my small-group leader. She lovingly pointed out I might need a little bit longer before I penned my sermon series. She was right. At the time, there was so much spite and sarcasm in that phrase. I thought I *did* know how things would turn out, and I was feeling all kinds of let down and hurt when things *didn't* turn out how I'd hoped. That phrase wasn't a joke to me—it was more of a lament. I attempted to conceal the hurt with sarcasm, but in truth, I felt incredibly sad and disappointed.

A couple months before *what I thought, was not* was born, we had just celebrated the new year. The beginning of a new year is always filled with so many hopes and possibilities. One of my favorite things to do in January is to come up with a word for that year. Choosing a word has proved to be very helpful and encouraging throughout the next 365 days. I also love that it sets the tone for the year, and it requires me to be intentional about setting aside time to ask God to speak to me about the upcoming year. It's always been an act of surrender to God to let Him lead the way.

This past year, a friend came over so we could dream and pray about the upcoming year together. In the past, I had chosen the word on my own, but this time I thought it would be special to choose one together with my friend. After all, sometimes it takes a really great friend to help you dream about things you aren't ready to say out loud. She shared words the Lord had given her for me, and then she prayed over me. As she prayed, I started to get more excited than I had about anything else in a really long time.

I had always longed for a "word of the year" to be something that would point to my future husband—something meaningful to me, so I would know this would be the year my dreams would come true. I needed God to throw me a small bone, letting me know I could trust in His promise to provide me with a hubby. I'm guessing God really loves when I ask Him for a word for the year and then decide what I want it to be before He has time to answer. As I'm sure you can guess, the word I longed to hear hadn't come yet. I was, however, already starting to feel like this year would be different.

My theory was confirmed as my friend explained she had asked

God for a word for me, and that word was *SPARKLE*. She also had bought me a new sparkly journal and penned a note on the first page that explained more about what the word meant. She talked about this year being my biggest adventure with God yet and how each twist and turn would be filled with much "sparkle." This was the year to shine, and it would be accompanied by lots of joy and fun. I was so ready for a year of light-hearted fun.

As I read her note, that word *adventure* resonated with me. The night before, I had a conversation with the boy I had been crushing on, in which we talked about wanting life to be an adventure, and I had written in my journal about it when we got off the phone. I know I can get easily excited, so that night I wrote about it as a way to give it to the Lord and not let it become a bigger deal in my mind. However, when I read the word *adventure* in my friend's letter, all reason and logic went out the window. I started jumping up and down and squealing. So much for keeping it together. To make matters worse, I have my reaction recorded. Because I know that everything that comes out of this friend's mouth will be powerful and meaningful, I had already pressed record on my voice-memo app as she began to speak and pray for me. I still flinch each time I listen to that recording. Hearing myself so excited about a relationship I thought was about to happen and now knowing it did not come to pass has been a difficult reminder.

At that point the dreamer in me completely took over. My first thought when she spoke the word *sparkle* was how engagement rings sparkle and, often, how wedding dresses sparkle too. Like I said before, I had a major crush on someone, and this crush had been going on for almost a full year. The timing wasn't right before this, so we were just friends, but I kept feeling like the wait would soon be over. I realize now this might have put a bit more pressure on this word. (I've always been so good at dreaming and jumping to all kinds of conclusions.) In my heart, at the time, the word *sparkle* and my friend's words about adventure all pointed in the direction I wanted.

I can run five steps ahead with the best of them and plan out a perfect future in my head—aren't we, as women, all good at that? In this case, however, my thoughts did seem to have some validity. I wasn't the only one who had started to notice something might be going on between me and this man. Mutual friends confirmed a few things I had already been feeling, which only made my mind race ahead even more. And things I had been writing in journals for years about my husband made total sense in this situation. As the days went on, my excitement grew. I woke up one morning, and my first thought was about another recording I had on my phone, so I decided to listen. I hadn't thought about that recording in years, but it was of a group of people from my church who were praying for me and asking the Lord to give them words to share with me about my husband. As I listened again to this recording, it amazed me how everything they had said supported what I believed I had already figured out. As I began the new year, I experienced much awe and wonder. I felt like I was following a treasure map, and each clue pointed to the same conclusion. Everything was really going to happen the way I had been dreaming it would for the last year. I was finally about to walk into my promised land.

You probably won't be surprised to know I thought I had the timeline all figured out as well. I had an idea in my head of when I would really see my dreams unfold and vividly remember thinking, *Wow. I'm so glad this season of singleness is almost over.* I wasn't sure if I could stand being single for even a moment longer than the plan I had in my head. I realize how crazy this all sounds now, but in the moment, I was convinced. Everything was so very realistic to me. I clearly know now I made way too many assumptions, but I just couldn't help myself.

As time went on, there were expectations I had that one by one weren't being met. Every time my phone buzzed, I hoped it would be a new text message from him, but it never was. There were so many conversations I hoped to have, but they never happened. When Valentine's Day came and went without a single word from him, I had to face facts. I had tried to prepare myself for nothing to happen that day, but I still had expectations. All the dream scenarios I had in my mind never blossomed into reality. Everything I thought I knew with such certainty fell apart in front of me. *What I thought, was most certainly not.*

I believe, in moments like these, the Enemy laughs and thinks, *We've got her where we want her. There is no way she will withstand another blow. This one will surely take her down.*

But there is always another voice. The voice of our heavenly Father, who lovingly says, "You will get through this. Take my hand. Trust me."

I did trust Him. I had walked through some deep disappointments already and somehow had made it to the other side. I believe it when James says, "Consider it pure joy, my brothers and sisters, whenever you face trials of many kinds, because you know that the testing of your faith produces perseverance" (James 1:2–3). I have watched that very thing play out in my life, so I knew it to be true, but I also knew the road before me wasn't going to be easy. We don't just get to skip the hard.

We also don't always see the gift in the moment, but there is a reward to walking through the difficult times of our lives. My gift from walking through the previous disappointments was understanding I *would* get through it—because I had done it before. I wish I could tell you I handled the new season of disappointment with grace and wisdom, that everything I had already learned was enough to keep me calm. But that wouldn't be true. At certain moments it was literally bang-my-head-into-a-pole bad. And yes, I do mean this literally. I imploded, and it wasn't pretty.

Thankfully, even in the midst of my outbursts, God was still faithful. He was always there and always willing to take my hand and help me through it. He's always ready and willing to extend grace. He's already paid a very high price for each and every one of our mistakes and is always there to offer forgiveness.

It's a strange feeling when reality ends up being so different from the plans you made. It forces you to rethink so many things. The one thing I quickly realized was it forced me to take a closer look at my beliefs about God. Even if I don't get what I want, is He still good? Is He still faithful? Do I still trust Him no matter what?

When we get everything we want, it's so easy to say we love God no matter what. But when we don't get that thing we prayed for, we are forced to decide if that is actually true. The natural question becomes this: Do I love God because of what He does for me, or do I love Him just because? I thought I already knew all these answers, but I had to take a deeper look into what I thought I knew. I had been preaching to anyone and everyone who would listen that God's timing was perfect and we could trust Him because of that. Over and over I found myself telling people I wanted God's perfect timing over my own. When I realized I would have to wait even longer, however, it was a huge gut check. Did I really want His perfect timing over my own?

As I began to dig into these questions and start some of my processing, I knew I would first have to deal with the disappointment. There was real hurt and sadness inside that needed to be addressed. I had learned from my previous experiences that ignoring those feelings wouldn't make them go away. I had also learned the longer I let the feelings fester, the harder it would be to deal with them later. The last thing I wanted to do was dig into the pain, but I knew there would be no other way to truly heal. So I took my disappointments to the Lord and asked Him to help me.

And the process began.

It felt very slow and tedious at times. Being a deep feeler is a blessing, but it also makes moving on extremely difficult. Plus, I wasn't fully ready at first to let the dream die. I wanted to hold on to the hope of things still working out for as long as I possibly could.

Throughout the years, my counselor has provided kind and gentle reminders about not skipping the grieving part. I've learned how vital that is, but I still don't like it. I know what grief looks like, and I know the hard that comes along with it. I also know the good that can come when I let myself experience the process. But that doesn't mean I like it. In this case, there were many things I would need to mourn. I needed to let this very specific and very real-feeling dream die. Letting a dream die means we accept the idea that the dream might never be resurrected or said another way: it might never happen. This part is so hard for me.

I realized I would also have to mourn each and every one of my expectations. Because I had so much of my future all planned out, I had to mourn those plans. I also had convinced myself that my season of waiting was almost over, so the last thing I wanted was to be back in that waiting place. I went ahead and let myself feel that disappointment too. I don't think I could have been in a headspace to accept where I was without first grieving all my dreams and plans.

I am no expert, but dealing with and mourning the loss included many things for me. I gave myself certain amounts of time to sit in my feelings. I knew it would not be a one-time thing, but I also knew, if I wasn't careful, I would end up sitting in the sadness so often that it eventually might consume me. After all, that's what happened last time.

This intentional time to feel my emotions usually involved journaling of some kind. I would give myself the time and space to write down everything I was truly feeling—not the pretty or churchy journal entries but the real and honest thoughts of a heart that was hurting. I would also share these honest thoughts with God in prayer. I know myself, and I know I often want things to sound pretty and cleaned up, so it's not always easy for me to be completely honest. Doing so, however, is helpful. Therefore, I really tried to spill my guts to God without holding anything back. I also processed in counseling and with some close friends.

Being completely honest with my close friends is such a necessary part for me, but it was still hard to admit I had gotten everything so wrong. The shame I was feeling was telling me so many things. It was telling me I was ridiculous and just needed to get over it. I also spent some time telling myself there was nothing even there to deal with. That it really wasn't that big of a deal. When we feel like the hurt isn't valid, we often try to downplay it in our minds. But if there is hurt there, it needs to be addressed in some capacity.

In this case, I hated admitting how sad and disappointed I was, especially since I hadn't even gone on one date with the guy. I eventually realized it didn't really matter how I got to this place of disappointment. All that really mattered was I was there, and therefore I needed to deal with what was really going on. The shame we feel can often keep us quiet. Letting people in, however, allowed me to continue to feel my feelings in a healthy space. My people gave me freedom to be sad but then also pointed me back to Jesus. They let me cry (and snot) all over their shoulders. They prayed over me and with me. They listened, to the point even I was sick of hearing the guy's name. And in the end, they even wanted to celebrate a job well done.

These friends helped me to see how far I had come and that this season had been a massive victory. When all I could see was how long I had waited with nothing to show for it, they saw it all as a test I had passed. I saw all the ways I was still getting it wrong, and it took me a while to see the good in this season. Eventually, I did start to see there had been victories. My previous disappointment had taken me so very deep down that it took me years to come out of that place. But this time things felt different. The same sadness and disappointment existed, but I felt much more equipped to handle it this time around. My friends helped me to see the growth I couldn't see at first. They also helped me to change my language and perspective. While I felt like I was now back where I didn't want to be, they saw it as a new beginning. Friends who can see beyond your flaws and still see all the good are the best kinds of people to have around. I needed them, and it felt nice to not be going through everything on my own this time around. This was another victory for sure.

Once I was able to start processing my emotions, it was time to ask myself some of the hard questions. I really believed all my hope was in Jesus and Jesus alone, but I had no way to know if that was really true until I didn't get what I wanted. It's one thing to say my hope is in Jesus but a whole different thing to have that tested and know it really is. As I dealt with the disappointment, I quickly realized part of my hope was tied up in getting that thing I wanted. In this case, it was the relationship. In my mind, there was so much joy and contentment connected to getting what I wanted. I always knew Jesus was the only one truly able to meet all my needs, but when I took a closer look into my heart, I realized it had actually become Jesus plus something else and not just Jesus all by Himself. It was helpful to learn that about myself. It showed me I needed to spend some time putting things back in their proper place—Jesus first and everything else after Him.

A few years ago, I was away at a women's conference with my church when many different kinds of thoughts and feelings rose to the surface. I had started the process of letting go of my best-friend ex, and it wasn't going so well. If you remember from earlier, there had been a lot of back-and-forth with this ex, which had made everything so much harder. I have all the journal entries from that time to prove just how not well it was going. During one of the sessions that weekend, I started thinking about how I have heard so many Christian women talk about waiting on God's *promises*. The *promise* of the job. The *promise* of a baby. The *promise* of a new house. The *promise* of our healing. Or in my case, the *promise* of my husband. I fully believe holding on to God's promises is a good thing, but when the promise of *things* becomes our entire focus, we lose sight of the most important *thing*. Jesus.

As I sat there thinking about all the things He had promised me, my thoughts started to get whiny (it happens so quickly). I wondered how much longer I was going to have to wait, when it was going to be my time to see God's promises fulfilled. The Holy Spirit interrupted my thoughts and whispered, "I am your promise." There was so much truth and love in those words. Jesus is my promise. He is my reward. He is the fulfiller of all my needs. His words didn't mean I couldn't dream and hope for other things, but that I could trust I already had everything I needed. That day at the conference, and then again in my most recent disappointment, I didn't get the answers I wanted. But I received the presence I so desperately needed. It was up to me to decide if I could believe that was truly enough.

At the beginning of this year, when I believed I was about to receive everything I had been asking for, one of my favorite songs had been "Goodness of God." The first time I heard it at church, it felt like my heart was going to leap out of my chest. As I sang about how God had been faithful my entire life, it was hard to contain my excitement. I believed I was about to walk into all His faithfulness, and I couldn't even wait. I pictured how so many previous moments were about to make so much more sense. I could see each heartache and failed relationship as a part of God's faithfulness as He led me into this new relationship. I could tangibly feel my heart beating so fast that day as I danced and sang.

We sang the song again at church after I realized the relationship wasn't going to happen. As soon as I heard the first notes, my heart sank. I could easily remember what it had felt like in January, and now it all felt so different. Could I possibly sing with the same enthusiasm I had the first time around? Was God faithful because He was about to answer my prayers for a husband, or was He faithful because that's just who He is? As I stood there, hands raised with tears falling down my cheeks, I told God I wanted to believe He was faithful always. But I would need His help to believe something like that. As I thought about it more and attempted to sing with true worship, my heart began to better understand that even today, while I was still single, God was faithful.

Another friend also helped me understand this a few weeks later. This friend had been trying to get pregnant for years, and doctors had told her it was basically impossible. But then she did get pregnant, only to miscarry the baby a few weeks later. That just doesn't make sense to me, and I'm not sure it ever will. But I will never forget what my friend shared that day. She was letting a group of us into her pain (which was a really beautiful moment in itself). Letting people in takes so much courage. As she shared her story, she explained how she believed God was good even in this situation. I'll never forget what she said that day.

"God's goodness and faithfulness will never be based on my circumstances. His goodness and faithfulness will never change, because that's who He is."

I knew that day if my friend could believe that with all her heart after losing her dream, I could hold on to that hope too. I knew she was so right. God was good, *period*. There could be nothing that followed that statement. He was never going to be "more good" or "less good" based on my getting everything I wanted. A good and faithful Father is just who He is. That is His character and that will never change.

What was hard to accept for my friend and also for me in my current situation, and something I am still working through, is I just might never have all the answers. I spent so much time trying to figure out what happened. I wanted to know what went wrong and wanted an explanation. I just wanted it all to make sense, but I eventually concluded that, in this case, I just might never know. Parts of me are still bound if I stay in a constant state of worry trying to figure everything out. I could drive myself almost to the point of crazy trying to figure out when my waiting will finally be over or how it will actually happen. I had to accept the hard reality that in my worry and discontent, I wasn't trusting Jesus like I claimed to. My need for clarity on what happened was a distraction from experiencing true freedom that is the result of trusting Jesus in all things. As we look to Him, march around our basements proclaiming His promises, surrender, let Him have our first love . . . that is when we start to achieve clarity. That is when our problems dim and the need for answers don't haunt us as much.

It was time to hand my desire for answers over to Him and trust Him more fully. He doesn't ever leave us in the dark to be cruel. If I didn't have all the answers, I could trust there was a reason.

I want you to know that even as I write this, not knowing is still hard for me. I still have this desire to know how I got it all so wrong. I still can't help but dream that maybe I didn't get it wrong. Maybe the timing just still isn't right. I still must give these thoughts to the Lord and let Him remind me that He, in fact, does have it all taken care of. He doesn't need my help. I think and often act like He does, but He doesn't need me to do anything besides trust Him.

There was a time my roommate and I had to move out of the beloved house we had rented for five years. We would have stayed there for years and years if the landlord hadn't decided it was time to do some renovations. As we looked around for other places, I started thinking about buying a house. Rent had gotten so expensive in Nashville, and it didn't make sense to keep paying so much each month. I could be paying toward a mortgage for the amount we were paying in rent. Even though it made sense, I quickly dismissed the thought. It had always been my plan to buy my first house with my husband. But I couldn't seem to shake the thought.

Eventually, I decided to take the first steps toward buying a house and just see what happened. I was amazed at how things came together. I started to get so excited as some of the details worked out. Soon, I was preapproved for a loan, which shocked everyone involved, and I began to see God's hand around every twist and turn. I hope by now you are noticing the pattern. I truly do believe God loves when I look for Him in everything, but then I often run ahead in my mind and create an entire plan. I did that with the boy, and I also did it with the house.

Everything was coming together according to plan, and I started looking at houses with my realtor. We eventually found a townhome that I thought was just perfect. It was newly redone, and I could see myself in the home. Everything was going according to plan until we were about to press send to put the offer in. At that moment, everything started to unravel and soon fell completely apart. No offer and no townhome. I became confused and frustrated, because I really felt like God had confirmed He wanted me to buy a house. With time running out and our moving date quickly approaching, my roommate and I went ahead and begrudgingly signed a lease for an apartment.

It wasn't until much later that I realized it hadn't actually been a good time to buy a home. My depression got really bad a little while after the house buying didn't work out, and I'm really thankful I didn't have the stress of owning a home on top of everything else I was feeling. I also realized the townhome I was convinced was my dream come true was actually in a part of town I didn't want to live in. Additionally, I was no longer excited about sharing a wall with neighbors. At that point in my life, it was a great idea since I was trying to escape reality and was never home, but it actually wasn't what I wanted long term. I didn't realize it at the time, but I need space so I can blare music and sing at the top of my lungs. And I love having people over and hosting parties. I'm pretty sure my neighbors in a townhome would not have loved this about me.

The whole situation has become such a beautiful reminder that God sees the full picture when I only see a part of it. While I was ready to race forward, He stepped in and stopped me from settling for less than His best.

Just like He always does, God did eventually fulfill His promise of a house. Three years later, I moved into my dream home. The space was more than I could ever ask for or imagine. Because it was a new construction, I got to pick out all the tile, paint colors, and the floor stain. The builders let me custom design a fireplace, and this house also has the basement of my dreams—complete with a home gym, which is something I dreamed about when I lived in the apartment I hated.

God came through with things I thought were only pipe dreams. I still look around my house sometimes and can't believe it's real. Especially knowing the journey it took to get here. Sometimes God doesn't have things go according to our own plans, because then we would be tempted to think it all happened because of something we did. God doesn't want to be reduced to a formula that we can figure out on our own. He longs to reveal Himself through things that don't make sense. And He invites us to trust Him despite what we see.

He took what could have been an ordinary house-buying experience, added three years of healing plus growth, and made a God-sized dream become an actual reality. I know this house is a gift from God and not because of anything I did, and so I can treat it as such. The thankfulness is richer, and I'm able to hold it with such open hands. I've been so much more willing to invite people into my home and not hoard it as if it were my own. The house is such a special reminder of just how much the wait was in my favor. The waiting was on purpose, and it was for my good. Most of the time we don't get to see the full picture, but it's such a special gift when God lets us see a glimpse of His plan.

I guess *what I thought, was not* actually never fell outside of God's plan. I'm certain if He once took my ordinary plans and turned them into something beautiful, He can absolutely do it again. Once we can realize that, disappointment and heartache no longer have the final say. God does. After all, each and every twist and turn is an opportunity to grow and learn to trust Him. It's always been about us looking more like Jesus and not just getting everything we wanted. I'm so very thankful He loves me way too much to give me everything I want when I want it. I can also say with so much confidence that this book would not be in your hands right now had the relationship started when I thought it was going to.

What God *knows* is so much better than what I *thought* I knew.

Let's Get *Real*

- What we think is going to happen is often not what God has planned. Have you experienced a situation when reality looked so different than your expectations? How did that feel? What did you do with that disappointment?
- Do you believe God is still faithful even if you never get that thing you want? Be really honest with yourself. If you are questioning God's faithfulness, know I have so been there too. Ask Him to begin to show you His faithfulness and to help you believe His promises for you are still true.

Dear Lord, I am realizing I so often have jumped ahead of you and created a series of expectations in my mind. I know when I jump ahead, it shows that I don't have complete trust in you. Will you forgive me? I want to believe that you are faithful even if I never get what I want, but I need your help to believe something like that. Will you show me your faithfulness and remind me that it isn't based on my current circumstances? Thank you for not giving me everything I want when I want it. Thank you for being the best Father and protecting me from walking into situations that aren't part of your best for me. Even as I wait, may my faith and trust in you grow.

Chapter 7

You Gotta Have Faith

I feel very strongly that I need to tell you this. I want all our hearts to take hold of this truth. You can dream, you cannot dream, you can pray, you can let it go, you can do all the right things, ask all the right questions, seek all the right counsel, and then, even then, sometimes it still won't make any sense. When that happens you just gotta have faith. Because a lot of the time, life just isn't going to make sense. There are some things that defy reason and logic. There are some things that have hurt so badly that you won't even want them to make sense. Even then, and maybe especially then, there is still hope. There is always something to cling to.

"But, Lauren, you don't know how long I have actually been waiting." I might not, but God does. Sometimes there is only one answer: you've got to have faith.

"Lauren, you don't realize that I'm getting up there in age, so by the time I get married, carrying a child might not even be possible." I get it, that's a terrifying thought. But I've learned you've got to have faith despite the fear.

"Lauren, what about cancer? That will never make sense." I agree, but the first step in those situations is trust God and have faith.

"But a baby is good and from the Lord, and we have been trying to get pregnant for years now." You're right, I can't explain it, but having faith is the only way to cling to hope.

"I found the love of my life and then lost him. That makes no sense." It sure doesn't. But even then, and I'd suggest especially then, you've got to have faith.

I don't say any of this lightly or with a lack of understanding or compassion for your circumstances. I, too, have cringed when someone has tried to throw the standard Sunday-school faith answer on top of my situation—especially when they have never walked through the same struggles. Even during the most painful and most difficult-to-understand times, however, we must cling to our faith and God's truth. There is no other place to turn. Everything else will eventually fail you. But God's Word never fails. God's truth is the way.

I love how one preacher I listened to explained faith. He said faith isn't an imaginary state where we convince ourselves nothing bad will ever happen. Instead, "faith is a focus." Faith is when we decide to put our focus on God and who He is no matter what—even while we are still going through the tragedy and even when the wait makes no sense. Even while the storm is still raging and there are no signs of it stopping anytime soon, if we can put our focus on God, we will develop this deep understanding of who God really is. He is not the God who just magically makes everything fall into place, but the God who is mighty to save even when everything feels like it is falling apart.

And here is the thing: we get to decide what we focus on. We can focus on God and the fact that He is for us, He is with us, and

He is working all things together for our good. Or we can focus on our circumstances. Personally, I have learned when I put my attention on my problems instead of Jesus, my faith shakes. Eventually, I find myself faltering. I begin to believe the lie that things will never get better, and before long, my emotions and actions follow along. I start making decisions based on the conclusion my mind has made instead of what the Word tells me.

I have also had to learn the hard truth that our circumstances are often far out of our control. I could never do enough to stop cancer from happening, I can't change the weather, and I can't will my husband to show up. Sometimes I would like to think I have more control than I do, but these things are far above my pay grade. What I choose to put my focus on, however, is something I can control.

Feeling tired, worried, stressed, and just all around over it? It's probably time to put your focus back where it belongs—the truth God has already spoken to you in the Bible.

I am fully aware that reading the Word will not immediately change your situation, but it will change the way you see your situation. When we can see things through the filter of God's love, we will see there is purpose to the pain. When we really understand His love for us, we can stop holding on to everything around us with such a firm grip. We can trust His love will always cause Him to do what is best for us. And He needs no help figuring out what that is. When we come up with a plan and then try to force everything to fit into that plan, we are only creating more stress for ourselves. God doesn't need any help with the plan or carrying it out. He just doesn't. He waits patiently for us to come to Him and hand over our fears, struggles, and hurts. His are the only true and capable hands.

When you can sit through the most difficult times in your life and still wait on God's timing . . . the reward will absolutely come! It might not look exactly like you thought, but it will come. It is in those moments when you rely on God as your guide you learn just how much you are capable of. What the two of you will be able to do together will be greater than you can ask or imagine.

This book you are holding in your hands right now is a beautiful reminder that God has a plan and can use all the hard times for His good purpose. I want the marriage, I want the family, and I long for things to look so differently. As you have read, I have tried so many times to force it to happen. I have tried to take control, and I have made decisions that weren't best for me, in my attempts to satisfy my longings. As I look back, I realize God has always had a plan. When all I saw was my hurt and my desire for marriage, He knew all of it would be used. He knew each moment of difficulty would form the words that would eventually become a book. And that book would be a beautiful way to help other women find truth even when life doesn't turn out the way they want it to. He redeems all of it, my friends, and even now, while you are still waiting, He has a plan.

Do you realize He has already given us everything we need to make it through this life? He has already spoken all the promises we will ever need to keep going. These promises are found in His Word. It is up to us to take hold of that truth. He provides the seed, but it is up to us to do the sowing. We must decide to take hold of the truth He has already spoken to us and apply it to our lives—again, to decide what we focus on.

Applying the truth found in God's Word is not something that comes naturally to me. It is something I must work on and practice over and over again. I have to stop what I am doing and make myself shift my focus, or applying His truth to my life often doesn't happen. A couple years ago, I felt as if I was entering a new season with my singleness. I had experienced so much healing from my depression and was walking in forgiveness from the Lord after all the mistakes I had made. I had learned my emotions and circumstances often caused me to ebb and flow in a very unstable manner. In fact, my emotions can change simply when I'm hungry! They are truly not what I want as the driving force of my life. If I wanted to stay planted and not be so wishy-washy, I would need a promise to hold on to.

I asked the Lord for a verse. I wanted a reminder that, no matter what, I could trust Him. I needed something I could keep going back to even when my emotions got the best of me, even as the days kept passing with no future husband anywhere in sight. I came across Jeremiah 29:11. "'For I know the plans I have for you,' declares the LORD, "plans to prosper you and not to harm you, plans to give you hope and a future.'"

I immediately told the Lord I didn't want that verse—such a Lauren move. I had heard that one so many times. That verse felt old. I wanted a new verse. He ever so gently let me know He hadn't misspoken. This verse was the one He wanted me to hang on to. (I'm so thankful God's so patient with me.) Before long, Jeremiah 29:11 started showing up everywhere. I saw this verse in journal pages I was writing on and in sermons I was listening to, and it kept coming to mind over and over again. Some college friends even showed up with a housewarming gift, which was a beautiful piece of artwork with that verse. These things shouldn't surprise me, but they always do. I obviously got God's message and soon fell in love with Jeremiah 29:11 all over again. If this was His promise to me, I wanted to make it my anchor when my emotions and circumstances tried to pull me in all different directions.

We should no longer be surprised when things try to come against the Word. Of course, the Enemy doesn't want us to take hold of the truth in the Bible. Of course, he is going to come after us with lies and try to keep us from taking hold of the promises of God. He knows how powerful it is when we really believe they are true. Time continued on, and I began to hear the whispers: *You know you are never going to get married, right? You know that each day that passes is another step away from being able to have kids. This sadness you feel today, you deserve to just stay there, because God hasn't kept His promise to you. You've earned the right to be discouraged. Aren't you tired of hoping for something that is never going to happen?*

It would be so much easier to just give up. Just stop believing God is going to come through for you; it will be much less disappointing that way. Then I envisioned another failed relationship, another disappointment, another holiday season alone with more friends getting engaged, getting married, and having babies.

But I had a choice to make, just like we always do. I could let all the hurt swirl around me and be carried whichever way my emotions blew me. I could fret and worry. I could make all kinds of false assumptions about who God is (which I have done countless times). Or I could go back to the promise He gave me.

In full disclosure, some days I stood strong on the promise, and sometimes, for weeks or months at a time, I sat in my feelings. But I am getting better and better about turning back to the truth before things really start to mess with my mind.

And so . . . as I walked into another friend's wedding alone . . . as I woke up sad and lonely . . . again . . . as the fear came rushing in, reminding me I wasn't getting any younger, I said my verse out loud—to the Enemy, to my mind and emotions, to the fear, and to the pain. "For I know the plans I have for you," declares the LORD, "plans to prosper you and not to harm you, plans to give you hope and a future."

I pointed into the unknown (yes, actually pointed), often with tears running down my cheeks, and declared that God had good plans for me. I reminded myself His plans have always been to prosper me and not to harm me. And that if He said it, He meant it, and it is true. Therefore, I could walk boldly and confidently into another wedding, into another day, and past the fear. When I take hold of the truth, fear can't win, and my emotions are less likely to get the best of me.

Again, standing on the truth of the Word doesn't just happen on accident. We have to be intentional about opening up our Bibles and asking God to speak to us. I am a very frail human with very real emotions, but I also know a very big and very capable God. This wonderful God has provided promise after promise in

His Word that I can turn to whenever I need it. And so I can still stand strong even when things are not going according to my own plans.

I've come to realize that God never wants us to have a life that makes Him unnecessary. If we were able to figure everything out, we wouldn't need Him. He doesn't do that just because He wants to feel needed, but because He knows what is best for us. And what is best for us is coming to Him for answers and putting our trust in something worth holding on to. There will always be some amount of mystery to God. We see the tiniest fraction of things and that tiny amount is blurry compared to how God sees things. God even spells it out for us in Isaiah 55:9, "As the heavens are higher than the earth, so are my ways higher than your ways and my thoughts than your thoughts."

Accepting this reality—that there are some parts to God that are always going to be a mystery—is going to be a part of all of our lives in one way or another. We get to decide if we can learn to take comfort in that or if this truth will bring more anxiety. At times, for me, it has been comforting to know I don't have to figure everything out on my own. To accept we will never be able to figure everything out can be so freeing. We can continue to try to force things to work out just the way we want, and we can stress about the timing and how it's going to happen, or we can let go. God doesn't ever force us—the choice really is up to us.

With that in mind, we can see the beauty of God's character. He doesn't get mad at us for questioning Him. He knows these truths are hard to grasp, and He wants an authentic relationship, which means He doesn't want it to be one-sided. I think He welcomes our questions because questions are just another way of inviting Him into our situation. I used to think asking questions showed a lack of faith. But even Jesus wrestled with questions. Right before He encountered the most difficult struggle of His life, He cried out, "My Father! If it is possible, let this cup of suffering be taken away from me. Yet I want your will to be done, not mine" (Matthew

26:39 NLT). Jesus, who was God's Son, asked if there was any other way. Ultimately, He answered His own question with "your will be done," but He still cried out to His Father for answers.

It's okay to not understand, and it's okay to ask for answers. That creates a true and honest relationship between us and our heavenly Father.

When I walked through my season of wandering, it would have been much easier if I had brought my honest questions to the Lord. Instead, I buried them, felt shame for them, and eventually came up with my own answers. Without even asking, I decided He wasn't good. I never gave Him a chance to show me He was.

When we come up with our own answers or make false assumptions, we show our lack of faith in God. I wouldn't recommend walking down that road. Ask the questions, and then wait for the answer. Sometimes we miss God's speaking to us, because we aren't still enough to hear Him over all the other noise in our lives. Dig into the Word so you can find the real truth. It's all there for you so you can learn who God is and the promises He has for you.

Sometimes there just won't be an answer. We all desire answers, and we all desire to be able to make sense of things. But sometimes the answer won't come, and there are many situations that will never make sense. We also need to know getting answers to our "why" questions probably won't bring the peace we are after.

When we don't get the answers we want, we must decide if we will trust God even then. Will we push past logic, just as Jesus did, and say, "Your will be done"?

There is a very sacred space that is not easy to find. It's a place of faith that believes even if God doesn't come through like we want or like we think we need Him to, He is still trustworthy and still good.

In the third chapter of Daniel, three young boys were faced with a choice. They could bow down and worship the king's idols, or they would be sent into a fiery furnace. They chose to walk boldly and confidently into the furnace. I love the words they spoke. "If we are thrown into the blazing furnace, the God we serve is able to deliver us from it, and he will deliver us from Your Majesty's hand. But even if he does not, we want you to know, Your Majesty, that we will not serve your gods or worship the image of gold you have set up" (Daniel 3:17–18). They knew who God was and what He was capable of. They believed He could save them. But they also took it a step further and said even if He didn't save them, they would not change their minds.

That is the kind of faith I want to have. That kind of faith pushes through the norm, pushes through my feelings, pushes through logic, and goes beyond my desires and fears. When we can do that, we can enter the sacred space where we trust God and want His will to be done above everything else. When we experience that kind of faith, we can say, "Even if I never get married, even if my earthly desires aren't met, and even if I never get to carry a child, God is still good." In that space, we realize who God is and who He has said we are. We trust Him enough to know that even if we don't get the thing we have always hoped for, it will still be well with our souls. I don't always have that kind of faith, but in the beautiful moments when I do, I experience a taste of the peace I will one day feel in heaven.

That kind of peace is worth fighting for.

Let's Get *Real*

- What is faith to you? Where are you practicing faith now, and where does it need to grow?
- How do you feel about the Word? Most of us know the "right" answers we should give here, but get deeper than that. Do you believe it has the power to change your situations? Does it feel stale and boring? Is it a struggle to spend time in the Word?
- What are the lies Satan is whispering in your ear? Are you agreeing with him, or telling him what truth is?

God, examine my heart and show me what is really in there. The rehearsed and polished answers are not going to get me to the places of healing I long to go. I pray that I can feel you close as I open up and show you what is really going on deep in my heart. I know there are areas of my life that I am lacking faith. I have such a desire to understand and for things to make sense. Will you show me how I can let go of those expectations and trust you? I also pray you would help me love your Word more. May it move past something I feel like I have to do to something I enjoy doing. I pray I would see it as a light in my darkest moments, and when I feel confused, would you remind me that all the answers I need are in your Word? Thank you for giving us the Word, which truly shows us how to live, and for your kindness in gifting us an example to follow.

Chapter 8

Remind Yourself of His Goodness

What do we do when the waiting feels like it has gone on forever and continuing to endure it seems nearly impossible? What happens when it feels like this season will never end? What if, in the end, all we can see is what we don't have?

The most honest parts of me have asked these questions many times. If you have too, how very real and honest of you to admit this waiting is difficult. If you have never admitted that before, now might be the time to let everything going on inside of you out. Now is when you are free to admit that it has been hard for you and extremely painful to wait. To operate in a state of health, we need to feel our feelings, but I would also be doing you a disservice if I didn't give you suggestions on what to do after that. Sitting in all the hurt, disappointment, and sadness is never where we were meant to stay. With that in mind, I want to provide real, practical, and honest advice.

If you are anything like me, when you are frustrated, your first reaction might be to tune any kind of advice out. Perhaps you decide the person giving the advice simply doesn't understand. I can't tell you how many times I've done that. You might be telling yourself I would never understand your wait and that you've already heard everything I am going to say. The truth is, I don't know how long you have been waiting, and I don't know what you have heard or haven't heard about waiting. But I do know my heart is for you and with you in this moment. So please, hear me out.

I think one of the first things we can do to move past the hurt is remind ourselves of God's goodness. This doesn't always come naturally to us but is an actual action step we must take. The truth I have learned over the years is I'm way more like the Israelites than I would care to admit. I read stories of their journey out of Egypt and judge them so harshly. Once things got hard in the wilderness, they began to complain. All that complaining put their focus on all the things going wrong, and eventually they decided they would rather be back in Egypt. Somehow, they had forgotten all the miracles God had performed to set them free. Once things got hard, somehow even being slaves sounded better to them. Again, I read their story with such judgment. *How could they forget all God had done for them? Wasn't parting the Red Sea enough to make them realize God was with them? Didn't they realize God had provided for each of their needs? So why were they even worried?*

I judge, but I am just like them.

One day I see God do the most amazing thing, and I rejoice. But the next day I question if He cares for me at all. I'm pretty sure if you are human you have been there. We are all quick to forget God's goodness. Our minds have all played tricks on us and made us believe that going back to our "safe space" would be better. Except that place isn't safe at all. It's full of hardship and pain. All we seem to remember, however, are the good parts of that difficult time. Eventually, going back to the familiar doesn't seem so bad.

I really do believe we have to remind ourselves of His goodness and what He has already done for us. It's just way too easy to forget. It's way too easy to focus on what we see right in front of us and miss how God is working behind the scenes. If we really wanted to, we could easily find no less than twenty things going wrong right now. We can decide we are sad, mad, or whatever, and then our mind can come up with all kinds of evidence to support that. But we don't have to give in to that. There is something we can do. We always have the choice to stop and remind ourselves of who God is and what He has done.

This lesson hit me hard a couple of months ago as I prepared to teach a message to a group of women at my church. This particular morning, I felt like I was in a funk, just not totally joyful and feeling kind of grumpy. I wasn't getting what I wanted, and I was frustrated and over it. As I began to prepare, I started to think about some of the things God had done leading up to this point in my life. The situation that stood out over all the rest was breaking up with my ex.

As I already shared, I was so mad and frustrated during that time. I just didn't understand why the relationship simply couldn't work out. It felt like I had waited long enough, and I was so ready to be married. I just wanted God to let me have this dream. As I sat there remembering, I felt God say, "I saw then what you couldn't see."

Man, was that so true. I could only see what was in front of my face and what I wanted, while God saw the whole picture. When my only dream was marriage and a family, God saw the speaking I would do, the Bible study group I would eventually lead, and He even saw this book in your hands. God said no to me because He knew it wasn't the time to settle down and move to Florida. If God had done that then, why would I ever think He wasn't going to take care of me now? He has always had a plan, and although it has often looked so different than what I wanted, He has always known better.

I have no idea if that story helped anyone else that day, but I know I needed to hear it. I needed the reminder. My own testimony had helped me look past my current feelings and put my focus back on Jesus. This is why it is so important to remind yourself of the great things He has already done for you. It might not change your situation, but reminding yourself of His goodness shifts your focus, putting it right back where it needs to be. Once that happens, you can begin to see that God wants good for you in everything, including your current situation. The hard part of today promises to be the foundation we will eventually need for tomorrow.

I promised practical tips, so I want to share some additional things that have helped me.

One of the most impactful ways I have been able to remember God's goodness is to *write it down.* Type it in your phone or put pen to paper. You could make a list, journal, or write a letter to God—the format doesn't matter. The important thing is to get those thoughts out. Write what God is doing and what He is teaching you. Then, later, when you are hungry and tired and convinced God has never done anything good for you, you can go back and read your words. We all need reminders. If you don't love writing, make videos. The first couple might feel weird. Trust me, I felt so silly at first, but I am so thankful for each and every video now. I can't even tell you how many times God has used them to remind me He is faithful. They have been the encouragement and hope I have needed to keep going. Making them and keeping a journal has also made me so much more aware of God and what He is doing. Our lives get so busy, so these moments to stop and remember are vital.

I have also learned that God is in the details. He knows I love them, and He uses them in such profound ways in my life. My videos and journal entries have allowed me to see such beautiful glimpses into how God is so specific and so personal.

On October 7, 2018, God reminded me just how detailed He is. Three years prior, I had not been in a great place. I had listened to a sermon in my car on the way home one night, and it had ended up being very encouraging and helpful. In truth, so much in my life wasn't going according to plan at that time. My car had broken down for the third time, I was living in a small apartment I hated, I had an eye infection that was causing all kinds of problems, and I was trying the entrepreneur thing, which also wasn't working out. On top of all that, the IRS was coming after me for thousands of dollars I owed from two years earlier. It seemed to be the perfect storm of things going wrong. I was broke, tired, sad, missing my mom, and desperately trying to get over my ex.

I had spent so much time wallowing in all that was going wrong, but something began to stir in me this night. I wanted to sing along to some country music on the way home, so I wouldn't have to think about all that was going wrong. Instead, I had somehow opened an app on my phone and saw a sermon titled "God Has Not Forgotten about You." I immediately clicked the link.

After listening, I had so many thoughts going on in my head. I sat in my car and started sharing them to my phone.

In the video, I shared how each day felt like I woke up to a mess. Over and over it was the same thing. I would try to gain a little footing, and then something else would happen. I explained how exhausted I was and how I just kept wondering what I was doing wrong. I believed God could do great things for other people, but it was so hard to believe it for myself. Plus, He didn't seem to be anywhere near me with everything that was going wrong. But this sermon message spoke the truth I so desperately needed to hear. I was reminded that night that God does have a plan for me, even in this. I know I didn't fully believe it at the time, and my emotions certainly didn't line up with what I was saying, but I still started speaking to myself anyway based on what I had heard in the sermon. Some of what I shared that night was that God would use this time in my life and my story to propel me into what He has for me in the future. There will be a purpose, and I would see it one day. I also shared I wanted to remember these moments so that I could relate and understand what other women are going through. I wanted my own mess to bring encouragement to others, which, in turn, would also help make it all worth it. I also always wanted to be able to remember how God took something that seemed so broken and used it for good. Again, I didn't fully believe the words I was saying, but I said on the video anyway, "This season won't last forever." I wanted this video to serve as a reminder of how far Jesus had brought me.

Three years later, on October 7, 2018, I woke up feeling nervous but also so excited. I was getting to teach to a group of women at my church that day—the first time I was doing anything like that, the first time I would share parts of my story, and the largest group I had ever taught. As I opened an app on my phone that shows me all the photos and videos I took on a specific day, I saw that video from three years earlier, and it blew my mind. Exactly three years earlier, I had made the video explaining how I wanted my story to be helpful to other women, how I knew God would redeem all the hurt and pain I was experiencing at the time. And now, three years to the day, I was sharing my story for the first time. I had been desperately trying to hang on to any hope I could find, while God had known all along what was to come. I bet He wanted to step in and make it all better for me, but He knew I would need the time of the hard and struggle. He knew it really would propel me. He knew I would stand before those women three years later, and they would need to hear my story. He had a plan for me. He had a plan for each woman in that room. He doesn't waste even a second of the pain. He redeems all of it. I never dreamed I would be thankful for all the hard, but I am. I saw in part, but He saw the whole picture.

Once we have focused our attention back on what God has already done, a natural response that usually follows is thankfulness. Again, we get to decide what we focus on, and whatever we focus on will grow. We can focus on the negative and how everything is going wrong—which will be the breeding ground for more frustration—or we can focus our attention on what we are thankful for and sit back and watch that action bear fruit. Once I start to focus on the good in my life, I start to believe more good things will happen. Then, my decisions and actions follow what I am thinking. Instead of making choices that lead to destruction, I start taking care of myself and making healthy choices. Again, what we focus on becomes the driving force in our lives.

Another natural response that flows out of a thankful heart is worship. I think we often utilize worship for our own benefit. When we really need something, we worship. But worship is not about us. It's about acknowledging God and His goodness. Although a natural result of worshipping is that we start to feel better, worshipping is truly about putting our focus on God. When we really do this, He becomes greater than all our problems. We realize He is a God of miracles and can turn any situation around. Nothing is too big for God.

I know maybe more than anyone that we don't always feel like worshipping. When we feel down, it is often the last thing we want to do. But I also believe that is when we need worship most. When you fight through your feelings and begin to worship in spite of them, you will find your spirit renewed. Pick a song, sing your own, or even just start speaking. Tell God who He is, say His Word back to Him, and tell Him what you are thankful for. I promise, if you do that for long enough, your perspective will change.

Another powerful way I remind myself of God's goodness has been to record voice memos on my phone when people are sharing encouraging words with me. I have no idea how you feel about someone giving you a prophecy but I know God longs to speak to His people and He uses other people to do it. It doesn't have to be weird or scary. When something does come up that seems like it could be from God make sure you write it down or do like I do and grab your phone to record what they are saying. This will also allow you to bring it to the Lord later since we always want Him to have the final say. He always confirms and follows up on prophecies. Also remember, if it is from the Lord it will never contradict His Word. Another thing I love to record is prayer. Sometimes as someone is praying for you God may give them a specific thing to pray for and you are going to want to remember it. Or maybe you are at a church service and the prayer feels just for you. Record it so you can listen to it again later. You could even record your own prayers so you can look back and see how God has answered those prayers. Sometimes I forget what I prayed, but looking back is a great way to see God has been at work the whole time. Even as I wrote this book, the Enemy tried to play all kinds of tricks on my mind, and multiple times I pulled up old voice memos to stir up my faith and encourage myself.

One prophecy in particular was from a couple of women I had never met before at a wedding. I was in the middle of dancing when they came and asked if they could pray for me. The first couple of times something like this happened to me, it felt uncomfortable, but God had used so many people to encourage me, so I was excited to hear what they had to say. I grabbed my phone and started recording. They started saying very specific and meaningful things to me, so I knew this was from the Lord. One of them ended up saying, "I don't know if you are a writer or you want to write." It had been on my heart to write but it felt like a far-off dream still. But she encouraged me by telling me God was going to give me the words and they would be used for so much good. You better believe whenever I felt like this book wasn't any good or worth sharing I stopped and listened to those words. I needed that reminder, many times over.

If you remember, previously I talked about how I asked God for a specific verse I could hold on to. This is another great practical way to remind yourself who God is and what He has already promised you. We must cling to the Word like our life depends on it. Let's be honest, sometimes our lives really do depend on it.

Find a verse that applies to your specific situation, write it down, put it in front of your face as many places as you can, and say it out loud over and over until you start to believe it's true. That verse is a promise from God for *you*. He has already spoken all the words we will ever need, and they are all found in the Bible. Use them, fight with them, and declare them over your situation. Your circumstances might not immediately change, in fact they might get worse, but it's in these moments we learn perseverance. And those are the times we gain strength as we learn to trust God despite what we see happening in our lives.

A friend once told me a story about how she'd had a conversation with God about holding on to the dreams she felt were still going to happen. She explained to God how exhausted she felt—as if she'd been dragging her dreams up a mountain. Because she'd been holding on to these dreams for so long, they felt like dead weight, and she started to think maybe she couldn't keep doing it anymore.

I loved God's response to her that day. She felt like He simply said, "How else are you going to get stronger?"

He was right. I've watched my friend grow stronger and watched her faith blossom through her struggles. I've seen firsthand the good that came from her struggle—a closer relationship with God. She has grown in her leadership skills and become someone many other women look up to. God has used her hardest moments for good.

What often happens is we read or hear something that impacts our heart. We find the verse that really speaks to us, or we hear the message intended just for us. We often feel emotionally connected to what we have heard. Those feelings help us feel strong, and we hit the ground running. We wake up the next morning ready to fight and excited about things changing in our lives. We read the verse or listen to the sermon again, and we pray. We feel so accomplished already. Some of us even go a step further and write the verse down on notecards. We make a plan to read the verse every day, without exception. We are really serious this time. Day two or three we wake up not quite as amped but still feeling pretty good. We tell ourselves this time will be different. This will not be like all the other times. This will be the time things really start to change. This time I'll learn to love my singleness, this time I will see God is all I need, this will be the time things turn around. And my personal favorite conclusion: then, I'm sure I will meet my husband right after that.

But then five days, a week, or maybe a couple weeks later if we are lucky, the new wears off and our excitement fades. We no longer *feel* different. Maybe we were wrong. Maybe this wasn't the moment when everything would change. We look around and notice that none of our circumstances have changed. The Enemy whispers about giving up hope. We believe him. We do feel disappointed again, and that doesn't feel good at all. Slowly, our old thoughts and actions creep back in. Sometimes we don't even realize it's happening. Those feelings are so familiar, they feel comfortable to us. Time begins to pass, and we eventually don't even remember what verse we loved so much. If we do think about the verse again, we feel shame for not sticking to our plan. We failed again. Why even bother trying again?

This was, and sometimes still is, me.

My counselor lovingly calls me "a deep feeler." Which couldn't be truer. I do feel a *lot* of things, and I feel them to the extreme depths. She often has to remind me being a deep feeler is not a bad thing, but it's something I must be aware of. My emotions often get the best of me. As I am feeling all the things, my emotions sometimes feel like they are bossing me around instead of me being in control.

Since I am a deep feeler, and since I have walked this road, I feel like I have the freedom to speak candidly. This is what I have found to be true: we have to stop letting our emotions get the best of us. Our feelings don't have the final say, and we can take control over them. Having faith and following Jesus cannot be based on our feelings. We might not *feel* like anything has changed, and we might not *feel* like God is good, but those feelings are often not what is true. We have to dare to believe that even though we don't feel different or feel changed, God is still able, and because of that, we can have hope. The choice is yours, and I want that for you more than anything. But no one can make you. You have to decide to hold on to the actual truth (found in the Word) and not just how you are feeling. I'm suggesting you look beyond your feelings, so you can see who God actually is. I want you to dig deeper and discover the promises God has already spoken. I want you to believe they are for you—not just lofty ideas but actual promises you can apply to your life and your circumstances. I want you to know when God says He is faithful, He means it. And when He says He will never leave you, it is true. Knowing that will help you stand strong as you face your hardest seasons.

One morning, not very long ago, I had to put all of this into practice. I really hope you are seeing I have a lot of hard days. You might be tempted to think that because I am writing a book, I have it all figured out. The Enemy might be trying to convince you that you are doing something wrong, because waiting *is* hard for you. Let me reassure you, you aren't. It's hard for all of us.

On this particular morning, I woke up feeling so sad and worried about how much longer I would have to keep waiting. As the tears flowed, I made myself get out of bed and went down to my basement. I wanted to do so many things in that moment that have not been helpful for me in the past. I wanted to call someone and explain my miserable life. I wanted to keep thinking about all the things going wrong. I wanted to crawl back into bed and go back to sleep. As I sat there crying, I knew those things, although they sounded comforting, would not actually help. Instead, I decided I would put on worship music, and I would write about the sadness.

As I wrote, I began to realize everything I was writing and feeling all centered around my situations and my emotions. Remember those things can be good indicators, but they are always changing, so they are not worth trying to hold on to. Instead, I decided to focus on those things I knew to be true no matter how I was feeling and no matter what was happening around me. I started making a list. This is what I came up with:

God is for me.
God loves me.
God wants the best for me.
God has a plan for me.
God is faithful.
The Enemy won't win. He never does.
God will never let me down.
God is my healer.
God is the meeter of every one of my needs.
God's timing is perfect.
God is working all things together for my good.
God will never leave me; He is with me always.

Once I started writing those words down, I felt better. I decided to take it a step further. I turned the music up even louder, stood, started marching around my basement, and started yelling these statements out loud. And then I yelled some more, and then I yelled some more, and then I yelled a little while longer until I felt even better. (Eventually, as it often does, it turned into a dance party.) If this all seems dramatic to you, let me reassure you, it was. But I have great news for you—it does not have to be this dramatic for it to be effective for you. You don't have to yell. You don't have to dance. I would, however, recommend getting serious about reminding yourself what is true. Use my list or make your own. Do whatever you have to in order to take control of your emotions. We have to speak these truths despite what we are feeling. We have to remind ourselves of His goodness even when things don't look good.

Again, I have no idea what you are facing right now. And I have no idea how long you have been in that season. But what I do know is this season isn't forever. There is hope. Even if you have failed a million times, today is still the day you can start again. Simply start where you are. Don't focus on trying to change everything in your life at one time. Just start somewhere. Pick a realistic goal for yourself and start there.

We often run ourselves into the ground trying to do it all. Start with one thing. Maybe spend five minutes in the morning in worship. Maybe listen to a sermon on the way to work instead of music. Maybe say one verse out loud each morning. If you quit on day five, go ahead and laugh at your humanity and start again on day six. Each choice you make to shift your focus to Jesus will be worth it. There will be a positive result to each and every action step you take. I have no idea how long it will take for things to begin to change, but I do know the change will be worth it. You will look back and be thankful for this season. You will be thankful God kept His word and eventually brought you out of that hard season. Every step is a process and there is purpose to each step you take.

Nothing from this chapter was written without the understanding that turning your mindset around is difficult. God knows it is as well. That's why He never expects you to do it on your own. He's already done all the heavy lifting for you. You must simply take hold of what He has already done. Know I'm right there with you, sister. I'm praying God meets you today, right where you are, and He reminds you it will all be worth it. He knows what your heart needs. I pray you would see even a sliver of light in the darkness and that you begin to follow it. May this be the start of a shift in your mindset to see His redemption story is for you too. This season and this time serve a purpose, and it might be the very thing He uses to propel you into all that He has for you in the future.

Let's Get *Real*

- Have you ever admitted that waiting on marriage has been hard for you?
- In this chapter, I gave lots of practical ways to remind yourself of God's goodness. What is one intentional thing you are going to do to help shift your mindset? Remember, you don't have to change everything at once, but you do have to start somewhere. So pick one thing.

God, waiting has been so very hard for me. I'm learning that is okay. You are in the hard too, and I believe you can use it. I've been having a really hard time remembering you are good. I feel like I have been fighting, but so many things feel like they have stayed the same. I want my emotions to match up with what I know to be true, but they just aren't right now. Will you remind me that you are good and you will use all of this for good? Will you show me there is always hope? Remind me of what you have done and what you have already brought me from. Show me practically how I can stay focused on your goodness instead of my circumstances. Thank you for loving me through all the hard and never leaving my side.

Chapter 9

You Are a Child of God

o you realize the God who created the entire universe is the same God who calls you daughter? Have you ever really stopped and thought about the fact that the one who put the planets in motion calls you His? It's pretty crazy when you think about it, but the God who has infinite resources and unimaginable power is the same God that loves you and longs to take care of you.

He's not just some lofty idea or far-off god. He's a god who is near to the brokenhearted (Psalm 34:18) and has already gone before you to make a way (Deuteronomy 31:8). He's personal, and He's intimate, and He loves you more than you could ever fathom. He doesn't just love you when you do everything right. He doesn't just love those we view as worthy of love. The truth is, there isn't a single one of us who is worthy. But He loves us just because that's who He is. He loves His children. That includes you. You are not the exception to the rule. You are the main attraction. He loves you so fully and so completely, and that will never change.

I know this is often a hard concept for me to wrap my head around. I've gotten so accustomed to the idea that I have to do things correctly or meet a certain standard to be worthy of that kind of love. I felt that way with sports—I believed if I had a really good game, people would be more proud of me—and I often feel that way with God. I act as if I have do something to earn His love.

But if our hearts can really take hold of the truth that God loves us no matter what, things will change. It's basically impossible to grab ahold of how much God loves you and remain the same. It is a process, but the way you see yourself, the way you think and your capacity to love other people will change. When we stand under that kind of love we begin to carry ourselves differently. We walk with more authority, confidence, and a whole lot more peace. God makes it very clear He has already accepted us. Even before we choose Him, He has already chosen us. No need to strive and no need to get it right all the time.

There is also nothing you will ever need that you can't find in Jesus. I know whatever you are waiting for is making you feel like there is a gaping hole, but there isn't. Jesus can fill that spot. He is the only one that can do it perfectly.

Trust me, this is not the just-get-over-it-and-trust-Jesus kind of explanation. This is the I-know-the-dark-lonely-nights and I-know-that-deep-seated-desire-to-share-your-life-with-someone-else kind of guidance. I get the hurt, and I get the longing. I've been there. I'm still there now. What I now know to be true in the depths of my soul, however, is those artificial dreams will never truly and fully satisfy.

My mind often plays tricks on me. I am often tempted to tell myself that finding a husband will be what makes me feel complete. That all of a sudden, things will just magically feel easier after the wedding. That once I am going through life with a family in tow, I will then experience deep joy and satisfaction.

But friends, the wedding, the husband, the kids . . . they can never fully satisfy. The best of the best will still not be perfect.

They, too, will let you down. Everything else will eventually let you down.

What can we do with this truth?

We can put Jesus in His proper place. We can let Him be the anchor. We can put all our hopes and dreams in His hands. When life or our emotions start raging, we can drop the anchor of truth and hold on for dear life. God is a perfect Father. He knows everything about you and still loves you. Nothing can change that. He will never let you down.

The Greek philosopher Heraclitus once said, "The only thing constant is change."[4] He was right. Everything in this world changes. Life changes, people change, the seasons change, and the weather changes (sometimes multiple times a day). We can't keep looking for stability in things that are unstable.

Even the best things this world has to offer will still let us down. I believe in the covenant of marriage, and I believe that once I get married, it will be forever. But I could do all the right things and marry the right guy, and because he's human, that man could still decide to walk away, to hurt me. That would be so horrific, but I know because Jesus is my ultimate hope, I could make it through that hard season. We live in a fallen world and are all imperfect humans, so there is literally no other person or thing worth tethering yourself to than Jesus.

Everything changes *except* God. He will never change. He makes this very clear in Malachi 3:6 when He says, "For I *am* the LORD, I do not change" (emphasis added).

Let that sink in . . . He *does not change*.

The same God who rescued the three boys in the fiery furnace and the same God who split the Red Sea to lead His people out of slavery is the same God who longs to be your hope today. What He was able to do then is the exact same thing He is capable of today. It's who He is, it's who He has always been, and it's who He forever

---

4   https://www.reference.com/world-view/said-only-thing-constant-change-d50c0532e714e12b.

will be. This God, who has all power and is perfect, is your hope. He is your stability when everything shifts around you. He is what you can cling to as you wait. He will never leave you. He will never disappoint you. He is bound to His word, and He is your constant.

This same God who longs to be your hope in times of disappointments or trouble has also called you daughter.

"You didn't receive a spirit of slavery to lead you back again into fear, but you received a Spirit that shows you are adopted as his children. With this Spirit, we cry, 'Abba, Father.' The same Spirit agrees with our spirit, that we are God's children" (Romans 8:15–16 CEB).

Adopted, by God Himself.

Can you even fathom it?

Friend, it's so very true. You are a child of God. You get to take on His name and walk with the same authority He has. For better or for worse, you are a part of the family.

Being a part of this holy family comes with an unlimited amount of benefits. "So you are no longer a slave, but God's child; and since you are his child, God has made you also an heir" (Galatians 4:7). The fact you are no longer a slave would be enough, but then God goes a step further and calls us *heirs*. Do you know what rightfully belongs to heirs? An inheritance. And in this situation, it's the most glorious inheritance you could ever hope to receive.

This is the other truth I want you to know. We must choose to take on this identity. God has already done all the work by sending His Son to die for our sins and give us a new name. He has provided everything we need, but He never forces us. In fact, this is a choice that must be made daily. We get to decide if we are going to focus on the things we don't have and sulk around or if we are going to walk in peace and joy, knowing God has already promised to take care of all our needs.

This is how we find contentment and joy in our singleness—by realizing we are already fully and completely loved just as we are.

No other human will ever be able to complete you. You must know in the deepest parts of you that you are good on your own.

If you aren't content now, you will not be content in marriage either. You will always just be looking to the next thing to meet your needs. Once you get married, you might have children, buy a new home, start a new job . . . always looking to the next thing to satisfy. That lack of contentment you feel now won't just change because you get married, have kids, buy a home, or start a new job.

We can't look at what we have or don't have to find fulfillment. We must stand on the truth that God has already given us everything we need. We are complete and whole *right now*. Even while we are still single, still longing, and still making a ton of mistakes. Yes, even here in the hard places we have everything we need.

Are you starting to see there is nothing you need that Jesus hasn't already provided for you? Like I said before, that doesn't mean you will get everything you want when you want it. No good father would give his child that. I'm not a parent, but I know I wouldn't give my child something that would be harmful to them. And I wouldn't give them something I knew they were not ready for. God is even better than the very best father this world has to offer. He wants to make sure He gives you the very best gifts.

Once you start to understand God will never withhold anything from you, you can start to see that the unmet desires can become beautiful gifts. If you don't have the husband yet, you can trust there is a reason. You can trust that even in the wait, God has a plan.

Once upon a time, over a very fancy meal at a local BBQ joint, I sat across from my small-group leader and cried into my mashed potatoes. She had just told me her prayer for me was that I would reach the point of being totally okay right where I was—that I would know God was faithful even if I never got my deepest desire. As the tears poured out, she asked me if I believed that was possible.

I explained, "I absolutely believe that is possible, but getting to that point means I would have to mourn my dreams and desires. And I would have to accept that it could take way longer than I want it to. If I say I trust God, that means I actually have to let go of my own expectations."

I knew I couldn't trust God fully and hold on to my plans and timelines at the same time.

A few short months later, my leader's prayers were answered. At church that day, we were singing "Here As in Heaven." One of the lines is this: "A miracle can happen now. For the Spirit of the Lord is here."

The person leading worship that day was really stirring up our faith, explaining that a miracle really could happen right in this moment. Things could turn around in this instant. People could be healed, and everything could change right now. She then encouraged us to reach up and take hold of our miracle.

Previously, whenever someone encouraged me to pray for a miracle, the first thought that always came to mind was my husband. After all the waiting and all the hurt, walking down the aisle would feel like a total miracle. And carrying a child? That also would feel like a massive miracle.

But on this day, my first thought wasn't the husband.

Before I had time to think, I basically grabbed toward where my heart is located and lifted it up to the Lord. I even shocked myself.

The miracle I received that day wasn't the husband (or even the hope of him). The exchange that happened that day as I lifted my old heart up to the Lord and received a new one was the true miracle. The old heart was full of so much hurt and so much longing. But this new heart . . . it is filled with so much trust that Jesus really is enough.

Since then, I have started to see that even without the husband and without the family, I am going to be okay because I already have everything I truly need. I have gained a new heart that trusts that God is good, and He is faithful no matter what. It's not that I will always get everything I want, but I can trust Him even more when I don't. The true miracle was for the deepest part of me to know (not just to *say* I know, but to feel it deep in my bones) that God is good.

I don't think it's wrong to still ask for the husband or to believe he is coming. I still ask. But I've watched my prayers turn from desperate pleas to words rooted in an unwavering faith. I still actually believe the husband is coming, but now it's no longer just about that. I know God has things for me to do in the meantime. This season is just as important as any other. Dare I say, even more important? I've begun to think beyond the longing into this glorious understanding that God has extraordinary things for me to do *right now*.

This deep faith tells me that if God has me in this place of waiting, it must be for a purpose. He must have a plan.

And that is how we thrive—not just survive—as we wait.

Are you willing to go there? Will you dare to believe that God is faithful even if the husband never comes? Would He still be good if His faithfulness isn't the story you've written in your head? Would He still be faithful if you had to wait even longer? What if the miracle you need isn't a husband but simply knowing that if what you hope for never happens you will be okay? What if you could thrive in this season instead of just survive?

Will you let the Lord take all the hurt and all the longings and turn them into something beautiful?

I know these are not easy questions and there are absolutely no easy answers. But know I'm here with you, praying you let Him do these things in your heart as He continues to work in mine. Let's take all the things that seem so broken and let them serve as reminders to a hurting world that God is good. Each and every crack and broken place could be exactly what is needed for God's light to shine through.

As you know, I love asking the Lord questions and then letting

Him speak to me. One day, as I sat in a hammock in the woods beside the cutest little treehouse, I felt God speaking these words to me. I believe these words are for you too, and I pray they bring hope and strength into your darkest hours.

> I want to be brought in. In fact, I long for it. My deepest desire is for relationship with you. Not to tell you what to do, and not to rule over you. But to walk with you and lead you to my best for you. Love will always be what my heart is tethered to. I want the best for you, always have and always will. You can trust that I know what I am doing. Even when it doesn't make sense to you, there is no need to worry because I have a plan. There are things that would be too much to understand and too much for you to carry. For your protection, I don't show you those things. I know that doesn't always sit well with your heart, but I need you to trust me. The love I have for you is more than enough, but you should also know there are certain desires I put in you, and I long to give you those things as well. I love you too much, however, to give it to you at any other time besides just the right time and at exactly the right moment.
>
> Those desires and those longings you feel . . . you don't have to ignore them or wish them away. But I also long for you not to see them as punishment. I am never going to withhold anything to try to hurt you. Those longings are a gift. They are a daily reminder that our human condition is frail and fleeting. And they are also a daily reminder that you need me.
>
> Again, my desire isn't to rule over you, but I long for you to come to me because I want what is best for you. I am the only one who truly knows what is best; I know you better than anyone else. My heart is always bent toward protecting you and not keeping things

from you. For this very reason, you can trust me with your heart. I know you have been let down in the past, but I am never going to let you down. I will never leave you or forsake you. Yes, you will walk through a storm or two, the world is not always a kind place, but even then, I will be with you, and I will make sure you make it to the other side.

If you let me, I will turn every tear and every ounce of the pain into something good. I will redeem it and create something better. I will never leave something the way I found it. I will always make it better. And when you feel like you can't possibly wait one more day, know that I am there offering you my hand. You can take it, and I will lead you home.

Each twist and every turn are all within my loving hands. I'm there in the hurt, and I'm there in the pain. I'm faithfully there cheering you on—reminding you with my Spirit and my Word that you can, in fact, do this. And when some of those things you are longing for come to pass, you will look back and be thankful for this time we shared. You are now more able and more prepared to care for that thing. And your appreciation for that thing . . . it has grown. Even before you walk into that destiny you so deeply desire, you will know my voice better, trust me more, and have more peace than you ever have had before.

Only then will you have learned what it means to walk through the fire and not get burned. Only then will you know firsthand that when I promise to be there with you in the deep waters, it is truth. And I guarantee there will be a little less fear. When you survive that season, you will know in the deepest part of you that you will be able to do it again. Then, your voice will be needed to encourage others—to remind them they are not alone and that you, too, know what it is like to wait. Show them compassion and point them to truth. You are an extension of my love to a world that really needs it.

Know that I am always here, and I am always fighting for you. The wait is a gift, and I will absolutely turn all the hard into something good. Know you can never change my love for you. I will always be here with open arms waiting for you to come home. You can always come home and fall back into my arms whenever you like. I will never force you there, but there will always be an open invitation. I love you. I am for you. I always will be.

Let's Get *Real*

- What would it look like for you to truly believe you already have everything you need?
- Could you believe God is still faithful even if you never got married?

God, thank you for speaking to me, and thank you for being so understanding of where my heart is right now. I know you don't expect me to be anywhere else but here. Because of that I can breath a little easier. Right now it still feels like something is missing. Will you show me I already have everything I need? Will you show me you are the one filling the hole even though it feels so gaping? I believe you long to speak to me, so I am here now, wanting to hear what you have to say. Thank you for loving me so perfectly and so unconditionally. I pray today will be a defining moment when I take hold of my brand-new heart. I'm handing you my bitterness, hurts, and unbelief and reaching for more of you instead. I walk forward this day believing you have a good plan for my life and a purpose for this season. Even though I don't see all the steps just yet, I know you are worth following. I'm choosing to believe what we are walking toward is better than I could ask or imagine!

Songs to Help You Through the Hard Moments

ongs have ended up being such a powerful and helpful part of my healing. So many times when I was feeling worried, confused, and frustrated, I found my way to a song. God used the lyrics of these songs to point me back to Him and remind me He was near. Along the way, I've learned that so many of these songs were born right in the middle of some of their writers' hardest seasons. It makes sense to me that you can't write a song that powerful without first experiencing the hard yourself. I found myself and my story in these lyrics, and they have provided hope when I needed it most.

Here are some of the songs from my "While I Wait" (yes it actually exists) playlist, and I pray they bring some encouragement to you as well.

"See a Victory"—Elevation Worship

This song has become my anthem lately, reminding me that God will never fail, and He will turn all the hard into good!

"Here Again"—Elevation Worship

I played this song on repeat at the beginning of the year. It has reminded me that I don't have to have it all together and that God has never once forsaken me. He will meet me right where I am.

"Over All I Know"—Vertical Worship

When I need to remember God is in control, this is one of the first songs I think of. He really is the God over all I know.

"Split the Sea"—Hannah Kerr

This song is a new fav. It reminds me that He can still do the impossible. No matter what I see, He can still split the sea.

"Yes I Will"—Vertical Worship

This is such a powerful reminder that the God who has never let me down before will most certainly not let me down now either. I also love that it talks about singing for joy even when our hearts feel heavy.

"Miracle"—Mosaic MSC

All of the miracles He has already done still mean so much to us today. This song contains powerful lyrics reminding us that because of God's love for us, we are all worthy.

"It Is So"—Elevation Worship

This song has helped me remember that when God says something . . . it is so. His promises are true, and even when I don't see them yet, I can still hold on to hope. If He said it, it is true!

"Confident"—Steffany Gretzinger

This song is another beautiful reminder of God's faithfulness. I also love that it reminds me that I can't win without Jesus. But He is there, and He is my hope and the rock I can stand on.

"Goodness of God"—Bethel Music, Jenn Johnson

As you have already read, this song has meant so much to me this year. My heart has changed as I have listened to these lyrics, and throughout the year it has taken on different meanings. But in the end, it has been the reminder that God has always been faithful.

"No Matter How Long It Takes"—Cross Point Music, Cheryl Stark

Oh man . . . this song. It was on repeat as I dealt with my most recent disappointment. It was hard for my heart to say, "No matter how long it takes." But deep down I still knew I was willing to wait. I wanted and still want to see Him show up in ways I can't explain. That just doesn't happen without some waiting taking place.

"Seasons"—Hillsong Worship

Seasons take time. God has a plan for all of them. This is another song that reminds me I want to let the waiting accomplish its full purpose. It will take time, but it will be worth it.

"Yes and Amen"—Housefires

God's promises are always going to be yes and amen. I need this reminder often.

"Heroes"—Amanda Lindsey Cook

Any song that talks about disappointment I'm so here for. But this one has also reminded me that I can dance despite those disappointments. They are used for my good.

"Take Courage"—Bethel Music, Kristene Di Marco
He's in the waiting. He hasn't forgotten or asked you to wait, to be cruel. I love this reminder that God is in the mess with me!

"Beautiful Story"—The Belonging Co, Mia Fields
If you don't know about this song . . . you need to. It's the anthem for single girls everywhere. It's a beautiful reminder that He uses everything for good, and He is already writing you the most beautiful story.

"He's Always Been Faithful"—Sara Groves
When I have doubted His faithfulness, I have gone back to this song. The lyrics remind me that He has always provided everything I need, and trusting God will always be worth the risk.

"Not for a Moment (After All)"—Meredith Andrews
When things in my life made no sense, somehow these lyrics always did. He is our constant, and He will never forsake us. This song is a beautiful reminder of that.

"Never Once"—Fellowship Bible Church
My sister and I both clung to the promises in this song the last time we learned my mom's cancer was back. There are scars from that season, but when I look back, I never once was left alone. And for that I am so thankful!

"Thy Will"—Hillary Scott
This song really carried me through after the loss of my mom. That will never make sense to me, but this song reminds me that I don't have to have it figured out. I can say, "Thy will be done" despite my confusion.

"Catch the Wind"—Bethel Music, Melissa Helser
Sometime, go listen to the story behind this song and how it came

about. It's been such a reminder that even when things don't happen like we think, God is still there. There is so much freedom when we believe He is good even when our circumstances don't look good.

"Do It Again"—Elevation Worship

God can and He will do it again. When the wait feels long and I forget, this song reminds me that I will see Him move again!

"There Is a Cloud"—Elevation Worship

This song has really reminded me that the hard is only for a season and the rain will eventually begin to fall. Also even the things I have planted with such a heavy heart will eventually spring forth.

"Defender"—UPPERROOM, Abbie Simmons

The lyrics in this song are so beautiful. I feel like in some ways they tell my story. When I thought I was totally lost, God still found me and put the pieces back together so much better than I ever could. He is the defender of our hearts.

"Right Now"—Cross Point Church, Mike Grayson

This is a song for those times you are questioning if God is really going to show up. Let these lyrics remind you that He always will. He is our fighter and Father, and He will finish what He started.

"Another in the Fire"—Hillsong UNITED

I played this song when I needed to be reminded there was some-one else in the fire with me. God always has been there, and He always will be.

"Never Lost"—Elevation Worship

God can do all things but fail, which means He has never lost a battle. That includes me and that includes this season. It has been on repeat since it came out, reminding me I can get through this and God will always win.